COPYRIGHT NOTICE

TEACH ME HOW TO BAKE

Dedication

This book is dedicated to Marshall & Cherrie-Amaya for being my first students in the kitchen. To my mother & father for journeying on the adventures I present.

This book is for all the Budding Bakers who dare to dream of bringing people happiness and joy through their creativity in the kitchen.

Thank You

Sharon Kinner, thank you for creating the Baking Buddies when it was simply just a dream. It took some time, but now we will share them with families all over the world.

Aamaal Anderson, thank you for your guidance, creativity and support with the layout and cover of this book.

To the test kitchen families who ensured I only presented recipes that worked with multiple age groups of children. Thank you, Kayleigh, Kingston, Royce, Lola, Vivienne, Elizabeth, Emma, London, and Stephen (and their parents)

Welcome To The Kitchen!
from Cocoa Cookie
Leader of the Baking Buddies Crew

HI THERE, SWEET FRIEND! 🍫
I'M COCOA COOKIE, THE FEARLESS
(AND FLOUR-COVERED) LEADER OF THE BAKING
BUDDIES CREW—AND I'M SO EXCITED YOU'RE HERE!

Welcome to Teach Me How to Bake! I'm **Cocoa Cookie**, and I'll be your guide (and biggest cheerleader!) as you learn how to bake with confidence.

Throughout this book, you'll meet my Baking Buddies, explore fun recipes, and pick up real baking skills one step at a time.

We'll help you stay safe, use the right tools, and learn what makes baking so magical.

All you need is a little curiosity, a clean pair of hands, and maybe a grown-up close by when things heat up.

Ready to mix, learn, and have some fun?

Let's bake something amazing together!

Sprinkling joy always,

Cocoa Cookie & the Baking Buddies

HOW THIS BOOK WORKS

This book is your guide to learning how to bake with confidence, one step at a time. It's not just about recipes—it's about learning how baking works so you can feel comfortable and proud in the kitchen.

Here's what to expect:

- **The Baking Buddies** will guide you along the way, each with a special skill to teach

- **Step-by-step photos** show you how recipes look while you bake

- **Skill Check-Ins** help you review what you've learned

- **Temperature Checks** let you reflect on each recipe and build real kitchen confidence

- **Fun science facts** and **mini experiments** bring the magic of baking to life

- **Safety reminders** make sure you're baking smart every step of the way

Work through the book at your own pace. Some days you'll read, some days you'll bake—and every page is designed to help you grow. All you need is curiosity, a good attitude, and maybe a grown-up nearby to help when things get hot or sharp.

Let's get ready to learn, laugh, and bake something amazing together!

TEACH ME HOW TO BAKE

Table of Contents

SECTION

1

BAKING BASICS
INTRODUCTION

BAKING BASICS: INTRODUCTION

Welcome to the wonderful world of baking! Before we get to the fun of frosting cupcakes or shaping cookie dough, let's take a moment to understand what baking actually is. Knowing the science behind it helps us become more confident in the kitchen—and trust me, understanding a little science makes your baking even better.

What Is Baking?

Baking is the process of using dry heat to cook food, usually inside an oven or over a hot surface. When we bake, we combine different ingredients like flour, sugar, eggs, and butter, and then heat them up to create something completely new. Cookies, breads, cakes, even roasted meats—those are all baked foods!

Fun Fact: The oldest oven ever found is more than 6,500 years old, discovered in Croatia! And the earliest grinding stones used to turn grain into flour?

They go back over 65,000 years in Australia. People have been baking for a long time!

BAKING BASICS: INSIDE THE OVEN

Who Is a Baker?

A Baker is someone who prepares food using baking methods. While most people think of desserts like cookies, cakes, and pies, bakers can also prepare savory dishes like baked chicken or roasted vegetables. If you've ever put something in the oven and cooked it, congratulations—you've baked like a baker!

What Happens When We Bake?

Let's use cookies as an example: When you mix your ingredients (butter, sugar, eggs, flour, etc.), you start with a bowl of soft, gooey dough. But once that dough goes into the oven, science takes over! Here's what happens:

- The butter and sugar melt and spread.
- The baking powder or baking soda reacts with heat to create little air pockets.
- The flour gives structure as it firms up.
- The eggs bind it all together.

And when it's done? That gooey dough is now a delicious, golden-brown cookie. Yum!

LOFT HOUSE
COOKIES RECIPE

Each time you follow a recipe like this, you're not just making cookies—you're doing science in the kitchen!

Your ingredients are changing at a molecular level, and YOU are making that transformation happen. Pretty awesome, right? **Let's look at this recipe for Lofthouse Cookies:**

EQUIPMENT

- Parchment Paper
- Baking Sheets
- Hand or Stand Mixer
- Sifter
- Parchment Paper
- Cookie Scoop, optional

INGREDIENTS

- ½ cup unsalted, room temperature butter
- 3 oz. cream cheese
- 1 cup granulated sugar
- 2 large eggs
- 1 tbsp vanilla
- 2 ¼ cup cake flour
- 2 tsp baking powder
- ½ tsp salt

LOFT HOUSE
COOKIES RECIPE

Ever wonder if you're mixing something the right way or if your dough looks how it should? That's where step-by-step photos come in!

These pictures show what each part of the recipe might look like as it's being made. From measuring and mixing to scooping and baking—seeing the steps can help you feel more confident before you even pick up a spoon.

Think of it like a visual map for your baking journey. You don't have to guess—you can compare your steps as you go.

Even if you're not baking today, use the photos to start noticing what good technique looks like. It's one more way you're building real baking skills!

LOFT HOUSE COOKIES RECIPE

- Preheat your oven to 350 degrees Fahrenheit.

- In a mixing bowl, cream together butter, cream cheese, and sugar until fluffy (approximately 5 minutes).

- Next, add the eggs and vanilla, and mix until fully incorporated.

- With your sifter, sift the flour, baking powder, and salt, then add them to the mixing bowl.

TEACH ME HOW TO BAKE

LOFT HOUSE
COOKIES RECIPE

- Mix all ingredients until fully combined. Set aside.

- Grab your baking sheets and add 1 piece of parchment paper on top.

- With your cookie scoop, scoop even balls of the mixture (now dough) onto parchment-lined baking sheets. Be sure to give the cookie balls space to spread out.

- Once done, place baking sheets into the refrigerator and allow them to chill for 30 minutes.

- After 30 minutes, roll the cookie dough into balls and lightly mash down the tops with your fingers.

- Next, take your cookies and place them in the oven. Bake for 12-14 minutes.

- Once done, remove from the oven and set on a cooling rack.

- After cooling for 10 minutes, top with store-bought or homemade buttercream frosting and sprinkles, enjoy!

BAKING BASICS: INSIDE THE OVEN

What Just Happened in the Oven?!
You mixed your dough, baked your cookies, and now your kitchen smells amazing! But what actually happened to turn that soft, sticky dough into warm, golden cookies?

Let's take a quick peek inside the oven (no oven mitts needed!).

The Heat Got to Work: Once your cookies went into the oven, the heat started to melt the butter. That made your dough spread out and soften.

The Dough Started to Rise: Next, the ingredients in your dough (like baking soda or baking powder) helped the cookies puff up a little as they baked. That's what gives cookies their shape and texture.

The Outside Turned Golden: As your cookies baked longer, the outsides began to firm up and turn a little golden. That's when the edges start to get crispy and the tops look baked—not wet.

The Cooling Makes It Count: Even after you take them out of the oven, your cookies are still doing a little work! Letting them cool helps them finish baking and hold their shape.

Skill Check-In - Baking Basics

You've already learned so much! Let's take a moment to see how much you remember before we jump into our next chapter.

What is baking, and what are some foods you can bake?

_____

_____

What does a baker do?

_____

_____

What happens inside the oven when you bake your cookies?

_____

_____

What do step-by-step recipe photos help you do?

_____

_____

What are some of the tools bakers use to make cookies like the ones you just made?

_____

_____

TEACH ME HOW TO BAKE

BAKING BASICS: WRAP UP!

You did it, superstar baker! 🎉 You've just learned the basics of baking—from what it is to how it works, and even how to follow a recipe like a pro.

I hope you're feeling proud (and maybe a little hungry)!

Up next, you'll meet one of my Baking Buddy friends **Benedict Waffle**, our safety scout! He's all about helping you stay safe and confident every time you step into the kitchen.

So grab your apron, wash those hands, and get ready—because Safety First is up next, and it's going to be egg-cellent!

Let's go!

Are you having a good time learning all about baking?

i've got some sweet friends that will guide you throughout the book!

But don't worry, I'll see soon!

SECTION

2

SAFETY FIRST

A BAKING MASTERCLASS

Welcome To The Kitchen
from Benedict Waffle
The Safety Scout of the Baking Buddies Crew

HEY THERE, JUNIOR CHEF! I'M **BENEDICT WAFFLE**, AND BEFORE YOU CRACK A SINGLE EGG OR TURN ON THAT OVEN, I'M HERE TO MAKE SURE YOU KNOW HOW TO STAY SAFE.

The kitchen is one of the best places to be—but it's also filled with tools, gadgets, and hot spots that we need to know how to use safely.

Part of being a great baker is learning to observe your surroundings:

- Do you know what every tool and appliance does?
- Can you spot where the stove, oven, and sharp tools are?
- Are your counters clear and your hands clean?

In this section, I'll help you understand not just the rules, but how to move confidently through your kitchen—whether that's recognizing important fixtures like outlets, sinks, and stovetops, or knowing when to ask a grown-up for help.

We'll learn to spot potential hazards before they become problems, so you can focus on what matters most—having fun and baking something amazing!

Ready to become a Safety Star? Let's jump in!

TEACH ME HOW TO BAKE

RULES EVERY BAKER SHOULD KNOW

Wash Your Hands

Before you touch any food, wash your hands with warm, soapy water for at least 20 seconds (sing the ABCs while you scrub!).

Tie Back Long Hair & Roll Up Sleeves

This keeps your hair and clothes out of the way—and out of your food.

Use Clean Tools & Surfaces

Make sure your bowls, spoons, and counters are clean before you start. Clean as you go!

Handle Knives with Care

Always use a cutting board and keep your fingers tucked in like a "claw" when cutting.

Oven + Stove = Grown-Up Zone

Never turn on the oven or stove without asking for help from a grown-up.

TEACH ME HOW TO BAKE

RULES EVERY BAKER SHOULD KNOW

Wipe Up Spills Right Away

Spills can make the floor slippery. Grab a towel and wipe them up fast!

Keep Your Space Clear

Remove backpacks, books, and anything you don't need from your workspace.

No Running or Horseplay in the Kitchen

Stay focused when you're around heat, sharp tools, or busy counters. Save the dancing for after the baking!

Benedict Waffle's Safety Tip!

Before you turn on the oven or pick up a knife, pause and look around your space. Is your area clean and clear? Are your tools safe and ready to use?
Smart bakers always check their surroundings before they start. A clean, calm kitchen = fewer spills and more success!

RULES EVERY BAKER SHOULD KNOW

OBSERVE YOUR SURROUNDINGS

Before we jump into baking, it's important to stop, look, and notice what's around you.

Whether you're cooking at home, at a friend's house, or somewhere new, the kitchen is filled with lots of important tools and **appliances—**and some of them can be dangerous if we're not careful.

Safety comes first! One of the very first things chefs learn in culinary school is how to protect themselves in the kitchen.

With so many moving parts—like hot ovens, sharp knives, sizzling pans, and heavy dishes—it's easy to find yourself in a sticky situation if you're not paying attention.

That's why we take time to learn about everything in the kitchen before we prepare our first dish.

Knowing where things are, how they work, and when to ask for help keeps you (and everyone else) safe and ready to bake up something awesome!

TEACH ME HOW TO BAKE

KITCHEN ITEMS & FIXTURES TO KNOW

Cabinets & Drawers

Where pots, pans, bowls, utensils, and small appliances are kept. Open one thing at a time to avoid bumps or spills.

Countertops

Flat surfaces where you mix, prep, and assemble your ingredients. Always clear off anything you don't need—backpacks, papers, or clutter.

Fire Extinguisher

This tool puts out small fires in case of emergencies. Know where it is, but only a grown-up should use it.

Knife Drawer or Knife Block

Where sharp knives are stored. Never reach into a drawer without looking first—always ask a grown-up for help when using sharp tools.

Outlets

These are the spots on the wall where appliances plug in to get power. Always keep water away from outlets and plugs!

TEACH ME HOW TO BAKE

KITCHEN ITEMS & FIXTURES TO KNOW

Oven & Stovetop

The oven bakes food with heat all around, while the stovetop heats from below. Both get very hot! Always ask a grown-up before using either one.

Refrigerator & Freezer

The fridge keeps food cool, and the freezer keeps things frozen. Always close the doors tight after you open them!

Sink

The place for washing hands, food, and tools. Be careful—sometimes water can be really hot!

Benedict Waffle's Safety Tip!

Great bakers know their kitchen! Take a few minutes to explore your space and learn where everything is. It helps you bake safer and smarter

TEACH ME HOW TO BAKE

UNDERSTANDING KITCHEN STATIONS

In every kitchen, tools, appliances, and ingredients are organized into special stations—areas designed to help everything run smoothly, safely, and efficiently.

Each station has a specific job, whether it's for prepping food, cooking meals, or storing ingredients.

When you understand how these stations work and where they are, you'll be able to move around the kitchen like a pro!

This helps you stay organized, focused, and safe, so you always know where to chop, wash, cook, or serve.

Let's take a look at the five most common stations you'll find in most kitchens:

UNDERSTANDING KITCHEN STATIONS

Cooking Station

The hot zone! This is where the oven, stovetop, or other cooking appliances live. It's where food gets cooked, baked, or roasted.

Food Preparation Station

This is where the magic begins! It's the spot for chopping, mixing, blending, and combining your ingredients before they're cooked or baked

Service Station

Once your food is ready, this is where you plate it, pack it into containers, or get it ready to serve. Think of it as the finishing area!

Storage Station

This station holds all your ingredients and supplies. It includes the pantry, fridge, freezer, and storage containers that keep food fresh until you're ready to use them.

Washing Station

Here's where you wash your hands, rinse fruits and veggies, and clean your tools. This station usually includes the sink and drying racks.

WHAT TO DO IF YOU SPOT A HAZARD

Even in the kitchen, unexpected things can happen— **spills, broken glass, or something getting too hot**! But don't worry. Knowing how to stay calm and report a hazard makes you a **Safety Star** that others can count on.

Here's what to do if you see something dangerous:

Step 1: Stay Calm & Step Back

If you notice something unsafe (like a spill, fire, or broken tool), slowly step away from the hazard. If anyone else is close by, calmly ask them to step back too. No yelling, running, or panicking.
Instead, take a deep breath, stay steady, and be the leader others can follow.

Step 2: Find an Adult & Report What You Saw

Go to an adult right away and explain clearly what you saw.
Try to include:
- What the hazard is (a spill, broken glass, etc.)
- Where it is located
- Who was nearby
- When you noticed it

Any details help the adult know how to fix the problem fast.

TEACH ME HOW TO BAKE

WHAT TO DO IF YOU SPOT A HAZARD

Step 3: Don't Return to the Hazard Until It's Safe

Stay away from the hazard until an adult says it's OK to return. Even if it looks safe, **wait for a verbal "all clear."**

Sometimes, extra steps are needed to make sure everything is really safe.

Step 4: Keep It Calm for Others

If other kids are around, don't spread fear or tell scary stories about what happened.

Let the adult in charge handle it, and show others how to stay calm and focused, just like a true Safety Star.

Benedict Waffle's Safety Star Tip!

Staying calm is the BEST way to help in a tough situation. When you take a deep breath and follow these steps, you become the leader everyone looks up to!

Skill Check-In - Kitchen Safety Terms

Let's test how well you remember the safety terms and actions we've learned!

Match each safety rule or kitchen item with the correct description.

Write the letter that matches each numbered item.

Terms & Rules:

1. Wash your hands _ _ _ _ _
2. Tie back long hair _ _ _ _ _
3. Ask an adult for help _ _ _ _ _
4. Wipe up spills right away _ _ _ _ _
5. Clean up broken glass _ _ _ _ _
6. Countertop _ _ _ _ _
7. Cabinet _ _ _ _ _
8. Kitchen appliance _ _ _ _ _
9. Outlet _ _ _ _ _
10. Ask for help _ _ _ _ _

Skill Check-In - Kitchen Safety Terms

Match each safety rule or kitchen item with the correct description.

Write the letter that matches each numbered item.

Descriptions:

A. Prevents slipping and falling in the kitchen

B. A section where food is plated or transferred before serving

C. Use the oven, sharp knives, or handle anything hot

D. Best solution when you're unsure, overwhelmed, or face a problem

E. Before cooking, especially after touching raw eggs or meat

F. Provides power to tools and appliances in the kitchen

G. Keeps hands and sleeves from getting caught or dirty

H. Equipment (usually electric) used to prepare food

I. Use a broom or dustpan, not your hands

J. A storage space for cups, bowls, small appliances, and more

SECTION

3

THE BAKER'S TOOLBOX – TOOLS & BAKING TERMS

A BAKING MASTERCLASS

Introducing Your Baker's Toolbox
from Honey Blu
The Baking Tools Expert of the Baking Buddies Crew

HEY THERE, BAKING BUDDY! I'M HONEY BLU—AND I'VE GOT A BUZZ-WORTHY JOB TO DO!

I'm here to guide you through all the essential tools every baker needs in their kitchen.

In Section 1, we talked about ingredients and a few of the tools that help bring them together. But now, we're going to take a closer look at these tools and learn how they help us bake safely, confidently, and like pros!

Tools are just as important as ingredients. Think of them as your baking sidekicks—they help you measure, mix, pour, and create all the delicious treats you love.

From spatulas and whisks to rolling pins and measuring cups, I'll show you what each tool does and how to use it like a real baker.

So grab your apron, roll up those sleeves, and let's explore the Baker's Toolbox together!

WHAT TOOLS DOES A BAKER NEED

BAKING SHEETS

Baking sheets are large, flat metal pans used to bake cookies, biscuits, and other treats. They help the heat spread evenly across the food so everything bakes the right way. Many bakers line their baking sheets with parchment paper to keep things from sticking.

GRATER

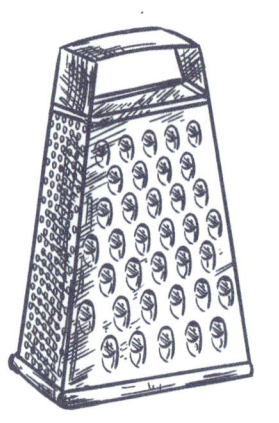

A grater is used to shred foods like cheese, chocolate, or vegetables into small pieces. It has sharp edges, so be sure to watch your fingers when grating. Freshly grated ingredients can add amazing flavor and texture to your baking!

HAND MIXER

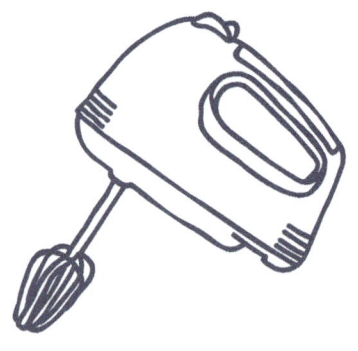

A hand mixer is a small electric tool you hold with your hand to mix batters and doughs. It has two beaters that spin when you turn it on. Hand mixers are great for smaller jobs like making cookie dough or whipping cream quickly!

TEACH ME HOW TO BAKE

WHAT TOOLS DOES A BAKER NEED

LOAF PAN

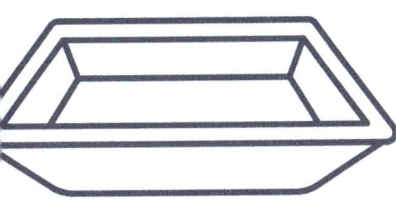

A loaf pan is a rectangular metal or glass pan used to bake breads, like banana bread or sandwich loaves. The high sides help the batter rise tall and keep its shape while baking.

KITCHEN SCALE

A kitchen scale measures ingredients by weight instead of volume. Some recipes are easier (and more accurate) when you weigh things like flour or chocolate. Just place a bowl on the scale, zero it out, and add your ingredients!

MEASURING CUPS

A measuring cup is used to measure ingredients like flour, sugar, and liquids. Dry measuring cups are used for **solids**, and glass or plastic measuring cups with a spout are used for **liquids**. Always level off dry ingredients with a flat edge for the best results!

WHAT TOOLS DOES A BAKER NEED

MEASURING SPOONS

Measuring spoons are used to measure small amounts of ingredients like baking powder, salt, and vanilla extract. Baking is a science, so even a small difference matters—make sure you level off each spoon for accuracy!

MICROWAVE

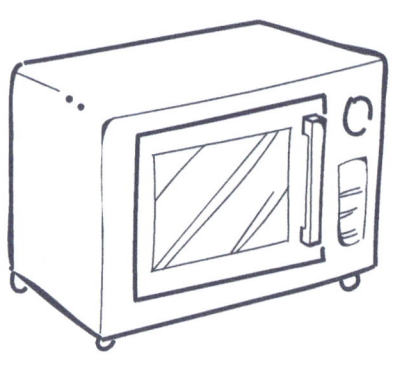

A microwave is a small oven that uses waves of energy to heat food quickly. It's great for melting butter, warming milk, or softening ingredients fast. Always use microwave-safe bowls, and ask a grown-up for help if anything gets too hot!

MIXING BOWLS

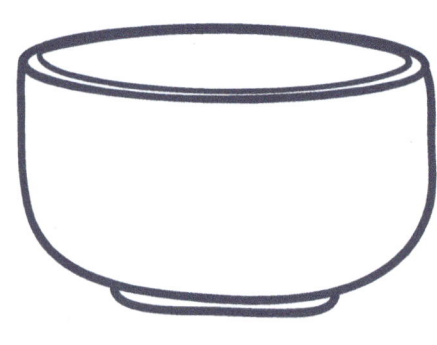

Mixing bowls come in lots of sizes and are used to mix, stir, and hold your ingredients. It's helpful to have a few different sizes when baking so you can keep wet and dry ingredients separate until you're ready to combine them.

WHAT TOOLS DOES A BAKER NEED

OVEN/STOVE

An oven and stove are the main tools used to cook and bake food using heat. The oven bakes things like cookies, breads, and cupcakes, while the stove cooks food in pots and pans. Always ask a grown-up for help when using heat—you want to bake safely!

OVEN THERMOMETER

An oven thermometer is a small tool you place inside the oven to check the real temperature. Sometimes ovens heat hotter or cooler than they should, and this thermometer helps you bake at the right temperature every time. It's a secret weapon for perfect cookies, cakes, and breads!

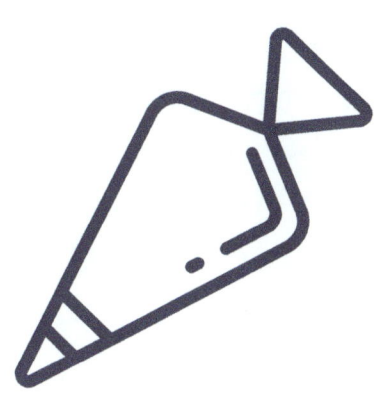

PIPING BAGS

A piping bag is a special bag used to squeeze frosting, batter, or cream into beautiful shapes. Bakers use them to frost cupcakes, decorate cookies, or fill pastries. You can also use a plastic sandwich bag with the tip cut off if you don't have a piping bag!

WHAT TOOLS DOES A BAKER NEED

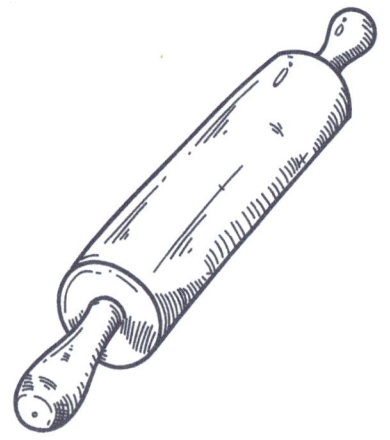

ROLLING PIN

A rolling pin is used to flatten dough for things like cookies, pie crusts, or cinnamon rolls. Always start in the center of the dough and roll outward for an even thickness.

RUBBER SPATULA

A rubber spatula is a flexible tool used to scrape batter or dough out of bowls. It's also great for gently folding ingredients together without popping the air out of delicate mixtures. No batter left behind!

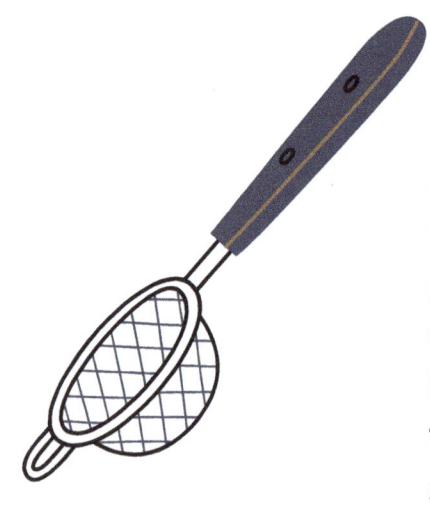

SIFTER

A sifter is a tool that breaks up clumps in dry ingredients like flour, cocoa powder, or powdered sugar. It also adds air, which helps make cakes and cookies lighter and softer. You can also use a fine-mesh strainer if you don't have a sifter!

WHAT TOOLS DOES A BAKER NEED

TUBE (BUNDT) PAN

A bundt pan is a round baking pan with a hole in the middle and fancy designs along the sides. It's used to make special cakes that look beautiful without needing a lot of decoration!

WIRE RACK

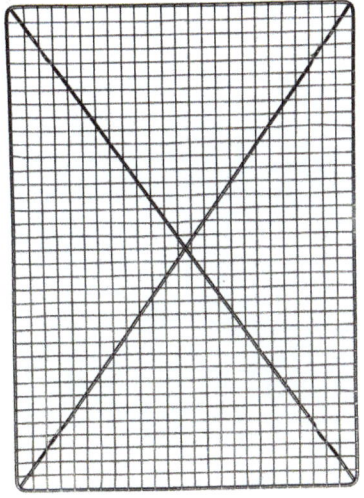

A wire rack is used to cool baked goods like cookies, cakes, or bread. It lets air move all around the food so it cools faster and stays crisp instead of soggy.

ZESTER

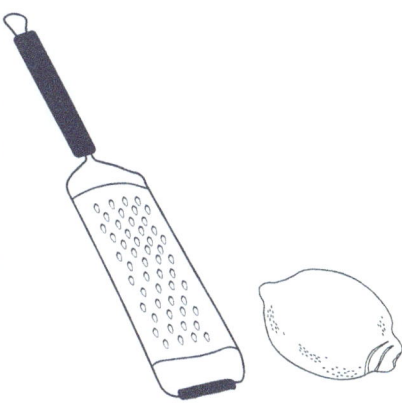

A zester is a small tool with tiny sharp holes used to scrape the outer skin (zest) off fruits like lemons, limes, and oranges. Zest adds a pop of flavor without the sourness of the juice. Always zest just the colorful part—not the white part underneath!

WHAT TOOLS DOES A BAKER NEED

SUGAR COOKIES

EQUIPMENT

- Parchment Paper
- Baking Sheets
- Hand or Stand Mixer
- Cookie Scoop, optional

INGREDIENTS

- 2 ¾ cups all-purpose flour
- 1 teaspoon baking soda
- ½ teaspoon baking powder
- 1 cup butter, softened
- 1 ½ cups white sugar
- 1 egg
- 1 teaspoon vanilla extract

INSTRUCTIONS

- Gather all ingredients. Preheat the oven to 375 degrees F
- Stir flour, baking soda, and baking powder together in a small bowl.
- Beat sugar and butter together in a large bowl with an electric mixer until smooth.
- Beat in egg and vanilla.
- Gradually add in the flour mixture.
- Roll dough into walnut-sized balls and place 2 inches apart onto ungreased or parchment-lined baking sheets.
- Bake in the preheated oven until edges are golden, 8 to 10 minutes. Cool on the baking sheets briefly before removing to a wire rack to cool completely

WHAT TOOLS DOES A BAKER NEED

Every baker needs tools. In this recipe, we use:

- Stand or hand mixer
- Parchment-lined baking sheet
- Cookie scoop
- Cooling rack

These tools help us mix, measure, and bake safely and evenly. Don't worry if you don't have them all—Cocoa Cookie and the Baking Buddies will teach you how to work with what you have!

Before you start baking, always make sure your tools are clean, working properly, and safe to use. A cracked bowl or rusty baking sheet can ruin your recipe and even cause a safety hazard.

Take a few seconds to check that nothing is chipped, broken, or dirty. If a bowl has a crack or your mixer isn't working right, it can cause problems in your recipe and leave you with a big, yucky mess. Remember, each step—and each tool—matters.

Just as important: **your workspace should be clear and safe.**

Remove bookbags, laptops, papers, jackets, or anything that doesn't belong in the kitchen. You'll need plenty of space to mix, measure, and move around comfortably.

BAKING TERMS EVERY BAKER NEEDS TO KNOW

A BAKING MASTERCLASS

BAKING TERMS

Batter

Batter is a soft mixture you can pour or scoop but can't roll out like dough. You'll use batter to make things like muffins, quick breads, cupcakes, cakes, and brownies. When mixing batter, stop as soon as everything comes together—**overmixing can make your baked goods tough instead of light and fluffy!**

Creaming Method

The creaming method is when you mix room-temperature butter (or another solid fat) with sugar until the mixture looks light and fluffy. This step is super important for cookies, buttercream frosting, and butter-based cakes. Creaming traps tiny air bubbles in the batter, making your baked goods soft and tender.

Cut-in Method

The cut-in method is used when you mix cold, solid fat (like butter or shortening) into flour until the mixture looks crumbly. This step is used for flaky recipes like biscuits, scones, and pie crusts.

Keeping the fat cold is the secret! Those cold pieces melt in the oven, creating flaky, buttery layers. Use a pastry cutter or two forks to cut in the fat—your hands can warm it up too much.

BAKING TERMS

Dough

Dough is a thick mixture you can roll, press, or shape with your hands. It's firmer than batter and is used for cookies, pies, biscuits, scones, and breads.

Because dough can dry out quickly, keep it covered if your kitchen is warm. And remember—gentle hands make the best dough! Over-kneading can make it tough or tear easily.

Folding

Folding is a gentle way to mix two things together—like whipped cream or fluffy egg whites with heavier batter. You fold carefully so you don't lose the air that makes baked goods light and airy.
 To fold, use a rubber spatula: cut down the middle, scoop underneath, and lift the mixture over the top. Turn the bowl and repeat slowly.

Tip: Add delicate ingredients a little at a time so you keep your mixture fluffy and smooth!

BAKING TERMS

Peaks

Peaks describe how firm whipped cream or whipped egg whites become as you add air. The more you whip, the **stronger** the mixture gets.

There are three types of peaks:
- **Soft** peaks flop over gently and barely hold their shape.
- **Medium** peaks stand up but curl a little at the tip.
- **Stiff** peaks stand tall and firm without bending.

Whipping Tip:
- Use cold cream for whipped cream (it thickens best when chilled).
- Use room temperature egg whites (they whip faster and stronger!).
- Cool cream, warm eggs = peak performance!

BAKING TERMS

Proofing

Proofing is the final rise that yeast dough goes through before baking. During proofing, the yeast releases tiny gas bubbles that make the dough puff up and become light and airy.

For the best rise, put your dough in a warm, draft-free spot (like near a preheating oven or on top of the fridge).

Proofing takes patience—but it's what gives breads, rolls, and pastries their soft, fluffy texture!

Softened Butter

Softened butter is butter that's been left out at room temperature (between 68–72°F) until it becomes soft but not melted.

It's the perfect texture for recipes like yeast breads, pastries, and cookies because it traps air, helping your dough rise and bake evenly.

To soften butter, leave it out for 30–45 minutes, or speed it up by cutting it into small pieces.

Tip: Don't melt it—soft is the goal

BAKING TERMS & TOOLS WRAP UP!

Awesome Work, Young Chef!

If you've made it this far, you've officially learned some of the most important tools and terms used in the world of baking. That's no small feat—go ahead and give yourself a big round of applause!

By now, you should be able to:
- Recognize your baking tools
- Explain what it means to cut in butter
- Describe how fermentation makes dough rise
- And so much more!

You're building real kitchen confidence, one skill at a time.

Before we move on, let's test what you've learned with a few fun activities!

Don't worry—the Baking Buddies will be right here to cheer you on.

Skill Check-In - Tools & Terms

SUGAR COOKIES

EQUIPMENT

- Parchment Paper
- Baking Sheets
- Hand or Stand Mixer
- Cookie Scoop, optional

INGREDIENTS

- 2 ¾ cups all-purpose flour
- 1 teaspoon baking soda
- ½ teaspoon baking powder
- 1 cup butter, softened
- 1 ½ cups white sugar
- 1 egg
- 1 teaspoon vanilla extract

INSTRUCTIONS

- Gather all ingredients. Preheat the oven to 375 degrees F
- Stir flour, baking soda, and baking powder together in a small bowl.
- Beat sugar and butter together in a large bowl with an electric mixer until smooth.
- Beat in egg and vanilla.
- Gradually add in the flour mixture.
- Roll dough into walnut-sized balls and place 2 inches apart onto ungreased or parchment-lined baking sheets.
- Bake in the preheated oven until edges are golden, 8 to 10 minutes. Cool on the baking sheets briefly before removing to a wire rack to cool completely

Skill Check-In - Tools & Terms

Let's see what you remember! Answer these questions on your own or discuss them with a grown-up baking buddy

What's the difference between a hand mixer and a stand mixer?

_____

_____

When should you use a rubber spatula instead of a whisk?

_____

_____

Why is it important to level your dry ingredients when measuring?

_____

_____

What does the cut-in method do to cold butter in recipes?

_____

_____

Can you explain what "softened butter" means and why it's used in baking?

_____

_____

SECTION

4

BAKING SCIENCE

FLOUR, SUGAR, EGGS AND LEAVENING

Understanding Flour, Sugar, Eggs & More!

with Bramble Berry

The Baking Science Guide of the Baking Buddies Crew

HI THERE, KITCHEN EXPLORER! I'M BRAMBLE BERRY, AND I'M *BERRY* EXCITED TO TAKE YOU ON A JOURNEY INTO THE SCIENCE BEHIND BAKING.

Sure, measuring and mixing matter—but what's really amazing is how ingredients like flour, sugar, and eggs work together to build the delicious treats we love. It's like a tasty science experiment every time you bake!

In this chapter, you'll learn:

- Why flour gives baked goods their shape and structure
- How sugar affects sweetness, color, and texture
- Why eggs are the ultimate multitaskers in the kitchen
- And how ingredients rise, fluff, and puff through a process called leavening

So grab your curiosity (and maybe a notebook), and get ready to mix a little kitchen chemistry into your baking. It's going to be egg-straordinary!

WHAT IS BAKING SCIENCE?

Have you ever followed a recipe step by step and watched your batter turn into cookies, or your dough rise into fluffy bread?

That's not just magic—**it's science in action**!

Baking is a kind of science called **food chemistry**. Every ingredient has a special job, and when you mix them together and add heat, they react and transform into something new.

- **Flour** builds the shape.
- **Sugar** adds sweetness and helps things turn golden.
- **Eggs** hold everything together.
- **Leavening agents** (like baking soda and yeast) help your treats rise and puff up.

Even small changes—like using cold butter or swapping brown sugar for white—can totally change the way your recipe turns out. That's why bakers follow directions carefully and learn how ingredients work.

When you understand the why behind baking, you become a more confident and creative baker.

Ready to learn the science behind your favorite treats? Let's go!

FLOUR: THE BUILDER

If you ask any professional baker what ingredients they use the most, you'll almost always hear: **flour, sugar, and eggs**.

That's because these three work together to build the structure, texture, and taste of almost every baked good.

Let's start with the ingredient that does the heavy lifting in baking—flour.

What Does Flour Do?

Flour's main job is to build structure in your baked treats.

Inside flour are proteins that wake up when mixed with water. These proteins link together to form something called gluten—a stretchy, elastic web.

That gluten traps little air bubbles and holds everything in place while your cake, cookies, or bread rise in the oven.

So basically:
- No flour = no structure
- Too much flour = dry and crumbly
- Just the right flour = baking success!

Mini Experiment: Which Flour Holds Its Shape?

Let's see how different flours absorb water—and how that gives us clues about gluten strength!

You'll need:
- 3 small bowls
- A spoon or a fork for stirring
- 2 tablespoons each of:
  - All-Purpose Flour
  - Bread Flour
  - Cake Flour
- 3 tablespoons of water for each bowl
- Paper and pencil to take notes

SCIENCE EXPERIMENT

Instructions:

1. Label each bowl: "AP Flour," "Cake Flour," and "Bread Flour."
2. Add 2 tablespoons of flour to each bowl.
3. Add 3 tablespoons of water to each bowl.
4. Use a spoon to gently stir each bowl for 10 seconds.
5. Let the mixtures sit for 5–10 minutes.

Now Observe:

Ask yourself:
- Which flour turned thickest and stickiest?
- Which one stayed soft and runny?
- Do any look stretchy like slime or dough?

Touch with clean fingers if you want—just don't taste them!

Why This Matters:

- Flours with more protein (like bread flour) form stronger, stickier gluten.
- Lower-protein flours (like cake flour) stay soft and can't hold as much water.
- This experiment shows why bread dough stretches and cake batter stays tender.

FLOUR: THE BUILDER

How does Gluten Work?

Gluten is what gives dough its stretch and chew. It forms when you mix flour with liquid and then stir, knead, or fold it.

- In bread: You want strong gluten to hold lots of air bubbles (hello, chewy pizza crust!).
- In cake: You want soft flour and less gluten so your cake stays light and fluffy.

The more you mix or knead, the more gluten forms, so that's why recipes sometimes tell you not to overmix.

What About Gluten-Free?

Some bakers don't eat gluten due to allergies or health needs. Instead, they use gluten-free flours like almond, oat, or rice flour.

Here's the catch: gluten-free flours don't stretch or trap air the way wheat flour does. That means they need help from things like:

- Xanthan gum
- Extra eggs
- Careful measurements

So if you're baking gluten-free, follow your recipe closely—and don't worry! With a little practice, gluten-free baking can be just as delicious.

TYPES OF FLOUR
BAKERS USE

All-Purpose Flour

Your go-to flour! Balanced protein = good for most recipes.
 Cookies, muffins, quick breads, pancakes—you name it.

Bread Flour

High in protein = strong gluten = super chewy bread.
Used for bagels, sandwich bread, pretzels, or pizza crust.

Cake Flour

The softest flour, with the least protein.
 Use it for light, airy cakes that melt in your mouth.

Pastry Flour

Lower in protein. Makes things tender and flaky.
Best for pie crusts, scones, or soft sugar cookies.

Self-Rising Flour

All-purpose flour that already has baking powder and salt mixed in. Great for quick biscuits and pancakes. **Don't use unless your recipe calls for it!**

TYPES OF FLOUR BAKERS USE

White Flour

Milled from only the endosperm. It's soft and pale in color. Great for cookies, cakes, and pastries that need a tender texture.

Whole Wheat Flour

Made from the entire wheat kernel (bran, germ, and endosperm). Adds fiber and a nutty flavor. Used for hearty breads and muffins.

Bonus Tip: Try mixing it half-and-half with all-purpose flour to make it lighter!

What Is an Endosperm?

Inside every grain of wheat, there are three parts:
- **Bran** – the outside shell (full of fiber)
- **Germ** – the tiny seed that can grow into a new plant
- **Endosperm** – the big, starchy center!

Most white flours are made from just the endosperm. It's soft, light in color, and full of starch—which helps give baked goods their fluffy texture!

TYPES OF FLOUR BAKERS USE

Flour Type	Best For
Bread Flour	Bread, Pizza Dough
Cake Flour	Light Cakes, Cupcakes
Pastry Flour	Pies, Pastries
All-Purpose	Everyday Baking

Mini Experiment

Mini Challenge: Flour Detective

Print or collect 3–4 flour labels from your pantry or store visit.
Can you spot the protein amount listed on the nutrition label?
It's usually around 9g–13g per serving.
Lower protein = softer flour. Higher protein = chewier bakes.

SUGAR: THE SWEET ENHANCER

Understanding Sugar

Sugar does a lot more than just make things sweet!

In baking, sugar helps create the structure, texture, color, and of course, the flavor of your favorite treats.

Different types of sugar—like brown sugar—can add extra moisture and rich caramel flavor, while others help cookies turn golden and crisp.

When sugar is heated, it goes through a special reaction called **caramelization**—that's when sugar molecules break down and change color and flavor as they cook.

This is what makes the tops of cookies turn golden and the edges of brownies chewy and crisp.

Sweet Science Fact

Sugar is made from a molecule called sucrose. While all plants contain sucrose, most of the sugar we use comes from sugar cane or sugar beets.

If your sugar bag doesn't say "cane sugar," it probably came from beets!

TYPES OF SUGAR BAKERS USE

Brown Sugar

Brown sugar is granulated sugar with molasses added back in.

- **Light brown sugar** = mild caramel flavor
- **Dark brown sugar** = deeper, richer flavor and extra chew

Use brown sugar when you want softness, moisture, and a little extra flavor punch—like in chocolate chip cookies and gooey brownies!

Confectioners Sugar (Powdered Sugar)

Super fine and fluffy! This white sugar is ground into a soft powder and mixed with a tiny bit of cornstarch to prevent clumps.

- Dissolves fast
- Best for **frostings, glazes, and dusting** on top of cookies or cakes
- You'll find this in icing recipes and buttercream!

Granulated Sugar

This is the **most common sugar** used in baking.
It's bright white, slightly coarse, and used in almost every sweet recipe—cookies, cupcakes, muffins, and cakes.

- Adds structure
- Helps baked goods spread
- Makes them golden in the oven

TYPES OF SUGAR BAKERS USE

Raw Sugar (Turbinado Sugar)

Light brown and coarse, this sugar has been minimally processed.
It has a light molasses flavor and crunchy texture.
Use it as a topping on muffins, pies, or quick breads when you want that sweet crunch!

Sanding Sugar

This sugar has big crystals and often comes in bright colors.

- Doesn't melt easily in the oven
- Adds sparkle and crunchy topping to cookies and cupcakes
- Often used for decorating holiday cookies

Superfine Sugar (Caster Sugar)

Finer than granulated sugar but not as powdery as powdered sugar.

- Popular in professional bakeries and in the UK
- Dissolves quickly—great for **meringues, whipped cream, or light cakes**
- A little hard to find in U.S. stores, but you can make your own by pulsing granulated sugar in a food processor

SWEET SCIENCE TEST

GRAB A GROWN-UP AND TRY THIS!

Instructions:

Make two small batches of basic cookie dough. In one, use only granulated sugar. In the other, use only brown sugar.
Bake and answer the questions at the end.

Equipment

- Parchment Paper
- Baking Sheet
- Hand or Stand Mixer
- Tablespoon or 1.5 inch cookie scoop
- Rubber Spatula or Wooden Spoon
- Cookie Cooling Rack (optional)

Ingredients

- 1/4 cup unsalted butter, softened
- 1/4 cup granulated sugar **or** light brown sugar, packed
- 1 large egg yolk at room temperature
- 1/2 teaspoon pure vanilla extract
- 1/2 cup plus 1 tablespoon all-purpose flour (spooned & leveled)
- 1/4 teaspoon baking soda
- 1/4 teaspoon salt
- 1/2 cup semi-sweet chocolate chips

TEACH ME HOW TO BAKE

SWEET SCIENCE TEST

Instructions

- Preheat the oven to 350
- Line a baking sheet with parchment paper
- In a medium bowl or stand mixer, beat the butter and sugar for 2 minutes until well combined.
- Add in the egg yolk and vanilla and mix well.
- Add the flour, baking soda and salt.
- Mix until just combined then cover and place in freezer for 10 mins.
- Scoop 1 ½ tablespoons of dough onto the prepared sheet, leaving space between each cookie.
- Bake for 10-12 mins, or until the edges are lightly golden.
- Allow to cool for 5-10 min

Comparison Questions

Which cookie is chewier?
Which one spreads more?
Which one browns faster?

Hint: **Brown sugar** adds moisture and chewiness.
Granulated sugar gives crisp edges and a lighter color!

EGGS:
THE SUPER BINDER

Understanding Eggs in Baking

Eggs are small—but in baking, they do BIG things!
They help:

- **Bind** ingredients together so your cookies don't crumble
- **Trap air** so your cakes rise and stay fluffy
- **Add richness** to recipes like cakes, cookies, and breads

Storing Eggs the Right Way

When you buy eggs from the grocery store, they should always be kept in the fridge and used within 3–5 weeks.

If your eggs come straight from a farm and haven't been refrigerated, they can <u>stay at room temperature</u> for a short time—but be careful! Leaving them out too long can make them spoil faster.

Baking Buddy Tip

Need your eggs to warm up fast for a recipe?

Place them in a bowl of warm (not hot) water for 5–7 minutes.

This brings them to room temperature safely without changing their "grade."

EGGS:
THE SUPER BINDER

Cooking & Baking with Eggs

Eggs need to be cooked thoroughly to keep your food safe.

When you're making French toast, quiche, casseroles, or anything with a lot of eggs—make sure the center of the dish reaches at least 160°F.

Use a <u>kitchen thermometer</u> to double-check when your food is ready. That's what pro chefs do!

Serving & Transporting Egg Dishes

Keep egg-based foods cold until it's time to eat. Here's how to stay food-safe:

- Serve cooked egg dishes right away
- Keep meringue pies and egg desserts chilled until serving
- At buffets or picnics? Keep egg dishes on ice
- Never leave eggs sitting out for hours—bacteria can grow fast!

<u>Special Note: Easter Eggs</u>

Decorating eggs for Easter? Make sure they're chilled before and after hiding.

If they've been outside in the heat for more than 2 hours, toss them out or use them as decorations.

TEACH ME HOW TO BAKE

EGGSPERIMENT

LET'S TEST WHAT HAPPENS WHEN YOU USE COLD EGGS VERSUS ROOM-TEMPERATURE EGGS IN BAKING!

You'll Need:

- 2 eggs (one straight from the fridge, one warmed in a bowl of warm water for 5–7 minutes)
- A grown-up helper
- 2 clear glasses or bowls
- A whisk or Fork

What to Do:

1. Crack one cold egg into a bowl.
2. Crack the room-temperature egg into another.
3. Try whisking each one with a fork or whisk.
4. What do you notice? Which egg blends more easily?

What's Happening?

Room-temperature eggs mix better and faster because the yolk and white are less firm.

Why is this important for baking?

That helps them trap air more easily—which makes cakes and cupcakes rise better!

EGG SAFETY

CHECKLIST

- WASH YOUR HANDS BEFORE AND AFTER TOUCHING EGGS
- NEVER EAT RAW BATTER OR DOUGH WITH EGGS IN IT
- USE A THERMOMETER FOR CASSEROLES, QUICHE, OR EGG DISHES
- KEEP EGGS IN THE FRIDGE UNLESS THEY'RE FARM-FRESH AND UNWASHED
- DON'T LET EGG DISHES SIT OUT FOR MORE THAN 2 HOURS
- AT PARTIES OR PICNICS, KEEP EGG DISHES ON ICE OR IN A COOLER

LEAVENING AGENTS: THE "LIFTERS"

Ever wonder how cupcakes puff up or bread rises into a soft, fluffy loaf? That's all thanks to **leavening agents**!

Leavening agents create tiny bubbles of gas in your dough or batter.

When those bubbles expand in the oven, they make your treats rise, stretch, and fluff up.

No bubbles = flat snacks. Big bubbles = bakery magic!

Why It Matters

Without leavening agents, your cookies wouldn't spread, your cupcakes wouldn't rise, and your bread would feel like a brick. (Yikes!)

That's why understanding which leavener your recipe needs—and how it works—is a key part of becoming a baking superstar.

LEAVENING AGENTS: THE "LIFTERS"

Chemical Leaveners

These are things you add to a recipe that cause a reaction and release gas (carbon dioxide).

- **Baking Soda** – Needs something acidic (like lemon juice or buttermilk) to work
- **Baking Powder** – Already has the acid built in, just add liquid or heat.

Biological Leaveners - Yeast

Yeast is a living organism! When it "eats" the sugar in dough, it produces carbon dioxide bubbles that make bread rise slowly over time.

- Used in breads, rolls, and pizza crust
- Needs warmth and time to grow
- Makes dough soft, chewy, and full of flavor

Mechanical Leavener

This type doesn't come from ingredients—it comes from you!

When you whip air into eggs or cream, you trap bubbles that help a recipe puff up while baking.

- Whipped cream and egg whites are great examples
- Used in soufflés, sponge cakes, and meringues
- You've got to fold them in gently to keep the air in!

TEACH ME HOW TO BAKE

MINI EXPERIMENT:
Which One Fizzes Faster?

LET'S FIND OUT HOW BAKING SODA AND BAKING POWDER REACT —RIGHT BEFORE YOUR EYES!

You'll Need:

- 2 small clear cups or bowls
- 1 tablespoon of baking soda
- 1 tablespoon of baking powder
- 2 tablespoons of warm water
- 1 tablespoon of vinegar
- A spoon
- A grown-up to help!

What to Do:

1. Label your bowls: One "Baking Soda" and one "Baking Powder."
2. Add the powders: Put 1 tablespoon of each into its labeled bowl.
3. Time to test!
4. **In the baking soda bowl**: Add 1 tablespoon of vinegar and watch what happens.
5. **In the baking powder bowl**: Add 2 tablespoons of warm water and stir.
6. Watch the fizz!
7. Which one bubbles more?
8. Did they react right away or need a little help?

MINI EXPERIMENT:
Which One Fizzes Faster?

LET'S FIND OUT HOW BAKING SODA AND BAKING POWDER REACT —RIGHT BEFORE YOUR EYES!

What's Happening?
- **Baking Soda** needs an acid to activate, like Vinegar or Lemon Juice
- **Baking Powder** already has acid mixed in, so it just needs water and heat!

This experiment shows why you can't swap one for the other without thinking—they react differently in recipes

Bramble Berry's Baking Buddy Tip!

"Not all fizz is created equal!"

If your recipe doesn't have anything sour or tangy, it probably needs baking powder, not soda.

Bonus tip: To test if your leaveners are still fresh, add a little vinegar to baking soda or warm water to baking powder—if it fizzles and bubbles, it's still good to bake!

TEACH ME HOW TO BAKE

Skill Check-In - Baking Science Review

What does flour do in a recipe—and what happens when it mixes with water?

_____

_____

How is brown sugar different from white sugar, and why does that matter in baking?

_____

_____

What are two reasons eggs are important in baking?

_____

_____

Can you name and explain the three types of leavening agents?

_____

_____

Why is it important to choose the right type of flour for your recipe?

_____

_____

BAKING SCIENCE WRAP UP!

You did it, kitchen scientist! Now that you understand how **flour builds structure, sugar adds sweetness and texture**, and **eggs bring everything together**, you've mastered one of the most important parts of becoming a confident baker—**knowing how your ingredients work**.

With these three power players on your team, you can create almost any kind of cookie, cake, bread, or dessert!

But wait—we're not done yet. Before you whip out the mixing bowls...

There's one more essential skill every baker needs to master:

Understanding how to read and follow a recipe like a pro.

Get ready, because in the next section, we're going to learn how to break down recipe cards, measure like a master, and prep your kitchen like a true baking boss.

Grab your apron—it's almost showtime in the kitchen!

SECTION

5

RECIPES: MEASURING MAKES A DIFFERENCE

A BAKING MASTERCLASS

Measuring Makes a Difference

with Logan Berry

The Measuring Maestro of the Baking Buddies Crew

Hey, future baking pro! I'm Logan Berry, and I'm here to help you measure like a master.

Measuring is one of the most important steps in baking—it's how we make sure every cookie, cupcake, and loaf of bread turns out just right.

A little too much flour or not enough sugar?

Uh-oh! That can really change how your recipe works.

But don't worry—I'll guide you through the best tips for measuring both wet and dry ingredients, so you'll feel confident every time you step into the kitchen.

Grab your measuring cups and spoons, and let's get started!

UNDERSTANDING RECIPES

We're off to a great start!

In the first few sections, you've learned about:

- The history behind the art of baking
- How to stay safe and protect yourself (and others) in the kitchen
- The tools and equipment needed to create delicious baked goods
- The science of baking with various flours, sugars, eggs and leaveners.

Now that you have a solid foundation, it's time to take the next big step:

Opening a cookbook and trying your hand at your very first recipe!

Take a look at the sample recipe for a Classic Chocolate Chip Cookie on the next page.

UNDERSTANDING RECIPES

INGREDIENTS

- 2 1/4 cups all-purpose flour
- 1 teaspoon baking soda
- 1 teaspoon salt
- 1 cup (2 sticks) butter, softened
- 3/4 cup granulated sugar
- 3/4 cup packed brown sugar
- 1 teaspoon vanilla extract
- 2 large eggs
- 2 cups (12-ounce package) NESTLÉ® TOLL HOUSE® Semi-Sweet Chocolate Morsels

INSTRUCTIONS

- Preheat oven to 375° F.
- Combine flour, baking soda and salt in a small bowl.
- In a mixing bowl beat butter, both sugars and vanilla until creamy.
- Add eggs one at a time, incorporating after each.
- Slowly add the flour, beating in a little at a time.
- Fold in chocolate chips.
- Place rounded tablespoons' worth or 1-inch cookie scoops worth on prepared baking sheets.
- Bake for 9-11 mins or until golden.
- Rest on baking sheet for 2 mins, then transfer to wire rack to cool completely.

TEACH ME HOW TO BAKE

UNDERSTANDING RECIPES

Do you love cookies as much as we do?

Did looking at the recipe on the previous pages make you want to grab your apron and start baking right away?

If you said YES! without hesitation, you're not alone—cookies make us happy too!

But before we dive into mixing bowls and spatulas, there's one important skill every baker needs to master first:

Learning how to read and understand a recipe like a pro!

Apron on? Let's do this!

TIP: ADD A SMALL PIECE/CUBE OF BREAD TO YOUR COOKIE TIN/CONTAINER TO KEEP THEM FRESH!

UNDERSTANDING RECIPES

What Is a Recipe?

A recipe is a list of instructions that teaches you how to prepare a specific food.

A good recipe will tell you:
- The ingredients you'll need
- The equipment you'll use
- The step-by-step directions to create the final dish

After you read a recipe, you should know what to use, what to do, and whether you're ready to bake it successfully!

The Three Parts of a Recipe

Every great recipe has three main parts:
- Ingredients
- Equipment
- Instructions

If a recipe is missing any of these, it could be tricky to follow—or easy to mess up!

UNDERSTANDING RECIPES

How to be a great recipe reader

Before you bake something amazing, you need to master the art of reading a recipe!

Here's what the best young bakers do:

- **Read the whole recipe from start to finish before starting.**
(That way there are no surprises halfway through!)

- **Check you have all the ingredients and equipment.**
(Nothing's worse than realizing you're missing something important!)

- **Pay attention to small details.**
(Little things like "room temperature butter" or "packed brown sugar" can make a big difference!)

- **Follow the steps in order.**
(Skipping around can cause mistakes—even for grown-up bakers!)

- **Stay focused—and have fun!**
(The best bakers enjoy the process, not just the final treat!

UNDERSTANDING RECIPES

Let's take another look at the ingredients for our Chocolate Chip Cookies:

- 2 1/4 cups all-purpose flour
- 1 teaspoon baking soda
- 1 teaspoon salt
- 1 cup (2 sticks) butter, softened
- 3/4 cup granulated sugar
- 3/4 cup packed brown sugar
- 1 teaspoon vanilla extract
- 2 large eggs
- 2 cups (12-ounce package) NESTLÉ® TOLL HOUSE® Semi-Sweet Chocolate Morsels

Pay Attention to the Numbers!

Did you notice something important?

In front of each ingredient, there's a number—these are the units of measurement.

They tell you exactly how much of each ingredient you need.

If you guess, or forget to measure, your cookies might turn out flat, dry, or way too sweet!

UNDERSTANDING MEASUREMENTS

Now that you know how to read a recipe, let's take a closer look at one of the most important parts: measuring ingredients the right way.

Getting your measurements right is the **secret** to cookies that *rise*, cupcakes that *fluff*, and bread that *bakes* just the way it should. One wrong scoop can throw off the whole recipe—so let's measure like masters!

When we talk about "measuring," we mean using a standard unit (like a cup or a teaspoon) to show the size, amount, or weight of something.

In cooking—and especially in baking—**measurements are everything!**

If a recipe says to add ½ teaspoon of something, but you accidentally add ½ tablespoon instead, you can completely mess up the **chemical balance** of your recipe.

Your baked goods might taste strange, look funny, or even not bake properly at all.

Sometimes one wrong measurement means...starting all over again. (Oh no!)

UNDERSTANDING MEASUREMENTS

Let's Look at Our Recipe Ingredients Again:

- 2 1/4 cups all-purpose flour
- 1 teaspoon baking soda
- 1 teaspoon salt
- 1 cup (2 sticks) butter, softened
- 3/4 cup granulated sugar
- 3/4 cup packed brown sugar
- 1 teaspoon vanilla extract
- 2 large eggs
- 2 cups (12-ounce package) NESTLÉ® TOLL HOUSE® Semi-Sweet Chocolate Morsels

What You Should Notice:

There are two main types of **units** you see again and again:
- Cups
- Teaspoons

But something even more interesting happens when you look at ingredients #5 and #6:

Granulated sugar and light brown sugar.

We'll focus on those two next—and why how you measure them can change everything!

TEACH ME HOW TO BAKE

MEASURING SUGAR
LIKE A PRO

Take another look at these two ingredients:

- 3/4 cup granulated sugar
- 3/4 cup packed brown sugar

Did you notice something different besides the numbers? If you guessed the word "packed," you're absolutely right!

What Does "Packed" Mean?

When a recipe says "packed," it means you should press the ingredient down firmly into the measuring cup.

You push the sugar down, squeezing out the air spaces and making room to fit even more.

This is important because how much you pack affects how much sugar actually goes into your recipe!

Why Packing Matters

- Granulated sugar should be measured lightly—no squishing, no pressing.
- Brown sugar should be packed down tightly when the recipe says "packed."

MEASURING SUGAR
LIKE A PRO

If you don't pack brown sugar correctly, you might not add enough sugar—and your cookies could turn out drier, crumblier, or not as sweet as you hoped.

And guess what?

¾ cup of packed brown sugar could actually hold almost as much sugar as a full cup if you press it tightly enough!

Packing changes how much fits into the cup—and that changes your final results.

Why Reading a Recipe Carefully Matters

This is why it's so important to read every part of the recipe carefully before you start baking.

Little details—like whether to pack your brown sugar or leave it loose—can make a huge difference!

If you skip over a word like "packed" and measure lightly instead, you might not add enough sugar.

And even worse?

Your cookies could bake perfectly...but not taste the way they should.

In baking, even small mistakes in measuring can lead to BIG surprises—and not always the fun kind!

WET VS DRY MEASURING TOOLS

Should You Use the Same Measuring Cups for Wet and Dry Ingredients?

Good question—and the answer is NO!

Even though liquid and dry measuring cups hold the same amount, they are specially designed to measure their ingredients differently.

Using the wrong type can throw off your measurements without you even realizing it!

What's the Difference Between Liquid and Dry Measuring Cups?

Liquid Measuring Cups:

- Made of glass or clear plastic
- Have a handle for easy pouring
- Measurements are printed or etched on the side
- Great for things like water, milk, oil, and juice
- Usually marked in bigger amounts like 1 cup, 2 cups, or 4 cups

Tip: You pour liquids up to the right line, not to the very top!

WET VS DRY MEASURING TOOLS

Dry Measuring Cups:

- Made of stainless steel or solid plastic
- Shaped like little cups with handles
- Measurements are etched or printed on the side
- Perfect for flour, sugar, oats, and other dry ingredients
- Come in small sizes like ¼ cup, ⅓ cup, ½ cup, and 1 cup

Great Work, you're now a Measuring Master!

Way to go! You've learned how to read a recipe, measure like a pro, and understand why every step matters. That's a huge part of becoming a confident baker—and you crushed it!

But here's the thing about baking: the more you practice, the better (and braver) you get. So in the next chapter, you'll meet Graham C. Moore, who's ready to help you put all your new skills to the test with real recipes you can try at home.

Get ready to whisk, scoop, mix, and bake your way into confidence—because in baking, Practice Makes Perfect. Let's keep going!

Skill Check-In - Measurements

Let's pause and see how much you've learned about measuring the right way—because great bakers don't guess, they measure with confidence!

What's the difference between packed brown sugar and loose brown sugar? *Hint: Think about how tightly the sugar is pressed into the cup.*

_____

_____

Why is it important to read the whole recipe before you start baking? *What kinds of details might you miss if you skip ahead?*

_____

_____

How can you tell the difference between a liquid measuring cup and a dry measuring cup?
Think about shape, materials, and how they're used!

_____

_____

How do you measure dry ingredients like flour the right way? *Describe what tool you use and what you do after filling the cup.*

_____

_____

Why is precision so important when baking? **Bonus:** *Can you give an example of what might go wrong if you measure incorrectly?*

_____

_____

SECTION

6

PRACTICE MAKES PERFECT

Let's Explore Recipes

with Graham C. Moore

The Recipe Roadtrip Guide of the Baking Buddies Crew

Hey there, rising chef! I'm Graham C. Moore, and I'm here to help you put your baking skills into action.

We've learned about tools, ingredients, and safety—and now it's time to get those aprons a little messy!

In this part of the book, we'll be baking real recipes and checking in after each one to see what you noticed, what you learned, and how it all turned out.

I'll be by your side as we:
- Mix up classics like chocolate chip cookies
- Bake banana bread, cupcakes, and even quiche
- Take quick "Temperature Checks" to reflect on each baking adventure

Remember, every great baker started with a first recipe—this is yours.

Let's roll up our sleeves and get baking!

BEFORE WE START, LET'S REVIEW!

Benedict Waffle's Safety Tip!

- Wash your hands:
  Clean hands = clean kitchen.
- Gather all your ingredients and tools
  It's called **mise en place** (that's fancy
  chef talk for "everything in its place").
- Ask a grown-up for help with the oven
  Hot ovens need cool teamwork!

Logan Bramble's Recipe Tips

Real bakers don't rush—they plan,
prep, and then bake like champions!

Learn more at
teachmehowtobake.com/academy

GET READY TO BECOME A COOKIE MASTER!

This recipe starts with a **Master Cookie Dough**—one big batch of dough that we'll divide into four parts.

One dough. Four flavors. Let's bake!

Review the recipe below and create this on your own. Once completed, answer the questions in the "Temperature Check" section.

4-N-1 ONE SHEETPAN COOKIES

EQUIPMENT

- Large Mixing Bowl
- 4 small/medium bowls
- Rubber spatula
- Whisk
- Measuring Cups
- Measuring Spoons
- Parchment Paper
- Baking Sheet (18*13)

INGREDIENTS

- 1 ¼ cup unsalted butter, melted
- 1 ¼ cup light brown sugar, packed
- 1 cup granulated sugar
- 2 large eggs, room temperature
- 1 large egg yolk
- 1 ½ tablespoon vanilla
- 3 cups all purpose flour, scooped and leveled
- 1 tsp baking powder
- 1 tsp cornstarch
- ½ tsp salt
- ¼ tsp baking soda

4-N-1 ONE SHEETPAN COOKIES FLAVORS

CHOCOLATE CHIP

- ½ cup chocolate chips (any kind)
- Additional chips for garnish

BIRTHDAY CAKE/FUNFETTI

- ¼ tsp cake batter extract (optional)
- 2 tablespoons rainbow sprinkles

COOKIES N CREME

- ½ cup chopped Oreos
- Melted white chocolate + more chopped Oreos for garnish

DOUBLE CHOCOLATE CHIP

- ¼ cup chocolate chunks (bakers chocolate bar)
- ¼ cup chocolate chips
- 1 1/2 tablespoons dutch processed cocoa powder

OATMEAL RAISIN

- 2 tablespoons oats
- 2 tablespoons raisins

PEANUT BUTTER

- 2 tablespoons creamy peanut butter, melted

4N1 SHEETPAN COOKIES

SERVING SIZE: 24

PREP: 20 MINUTES

BAKE: 22 MINUTES

Gather all ingredients. Preheat the oven to 350°F. Spray a standard half sheet pan with nonstick spray (13×18) and set aside.

Add the melted butter and sugars together in a large mixing bowl. Whisk together until smooth. Be sure to break up any clumps of brown sugar.

Add the eggs, milk, and vanilla. Whisk until smooth.

Add the dry ingredients. Fold with rubber spatula until mostly combined. **Do not overmix the cookie dough in this step.**

Divide the base cookie dough batter into 4 equal sections and place in 4 small/medium sized bowls.

You can use a food scale to weigh each portion of so they are more accurate if you'd like, each quadrant will be about 10 oz each.

Add your flavor mix-ins to each bowl and mix just until combined.

Place each cookie portion onto a quadrant of your sheet pan.

Using a rubber spatula, flatten each section down evenly. The cookie dough should fill the entire sheet pan and the cookie doughs will be touching.

Add additional sprinkles on the birthday cake section. (You'll add extra Oreos or chocolate chips on AFTER the cookies bake)

Bake for 18-22 mins. Do not overbake. Once the cookies are out of the oven they will continue to bake on the sheetpan.

Cool completey, then cut into squares and enjoy! **Store in an air tight container for up to 5 days.**

Temperature Check: 4-in-1 Sheet Pan Cookies

What does "fold until mostly combined" mean, and why don't we want to overmix the dough? *Hint: Think about what could happen to your cookies if the dough is mixed too much.*

_____

_____

Which of the four cookie flavors was your favorite to make and why?

_____

_____

What did you notice about the texture of your cookies after they cooled? Did they puff up or settle down?

_____

_____

Which kitchen stations did you use while making this recipe? *Hint: Think back to Section 2—did you mix, bake, or clean up?*

_____

_____

BANANA BREAD

SERVING SIZE: 8

PREP: 10 MINUTES

BAKE: 75 MINUTES

Review the recipe below and create this on your own. Once completed, answer the questions in the "Temperature Check" section.

BANANA BREAD

EQUIPMENT

- Non-Stick Loaf Pan
- Medium bowl
- Large bowl
- Whisk
- Rubber Spatula
- Measuring cups and spoons

INGREDIENTS

- 2 cups all-purpose flour
- 1 tsp baking soda
- 1/4 tsp salt
- 1/8 tsp cinnamon
- 1 1/4 cup granulated sugar
- 1 large egg
- 1 tsp vanilla
- 1/2 cup vegetable oil
- 2 tbsp buttermilk or whole milk
- 1 cup mashed banana 3 extra ripe bananas
- 1/2 cup chopped walnuts inside batter
- 1/4 cup chopped walnuts on top

Gather all ingredients.
Preheat the oven to 325°F.

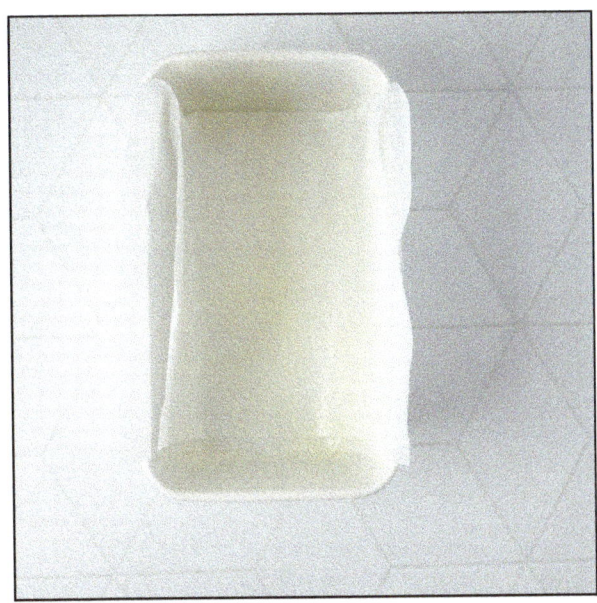

Spray the loaf pan with baking spray and then line with parchment (for easy release). Spray the parchment with non-stick as well and set aside

Whisk together flour, baking soda, salt, and cinnamon in a medium-sized bowl, then set aside

Add the egg, vanilla, sugar, and vegetable oil in a larger bowl and whisk together.

Pour dry ingredients into the wet ingredients bowl and, using a rubber spatula carefully mix together. (It will be coarse and dry at this point- don't over mix).

Mash the bananas and add them to the bowl.

Add buttermilk (or whole milk) and 1/2 cup chopped walnuts

Mix well with the rubber spatula, making sure to scrape the bottom of the bowl.

Once everything is well incorporated (no dry flour left) pour into the prepared pan.

Top with 1/4 cup walnuts
Bake for 75 mins (begin checking around the 55 min mark)

Baking Buddy Tip

Banana bread takes patience—and that's a baker's secret weapon!

- Check your bread with a toothpick: if it comes out clean or with just a few crumbs, it's done.
- Let it cool before slicing—it keeps the inside moist and delicious.
- Extra bananas? Freeze them for next time!

Temperature Check:
Classic Banana Bread

Why do we mash the bananas before adding them to the batter instead of adding them whole? *Hint: Think about mixing and texture!*

_____

_____

What tool did you use to combine the dry and wet ingredients—and why is it important not to overmix?

_____

_____

What did your banana bread look, smell, or feel like when it came out of the oven? *Was it golden? Did the top feel firm? How did it smell?*

_____

_____

Did you use buttermilk or whole milk in your batter? How do you think it helped the bread?

_____

_____

TEACH ME HOW TO BAKE

DOUBLE CHUNK BROWNIES

SERVING SIZE: 8

PREP: 10 MINUTES

BAKE: 30 MINUTES

Review the recipe below and create this on your own. Once completed, answer the questions in the "Temperature Check" section.

DOUBLE CHUNK BROWNIES

EQUIPMENT

- 8x8-inch baking dish
- Parchment paper or non-stick baking spray
- Medium-large bowl
- Whisk
- Rubber spatula
- Sifter or fine-mesh strainer

INGREDIENTS

- ½ cup (1 stick) unsalted butter, melted
- 1 cup granulated sugar
- 2 large eggs (room temperature)
- 2 teaspoons vanilla extract
- ¾ cup all-purpose flour (scooped and leveled)
- ½ cup cocoa powder
- ¼ teaspoon salt
- 2 cups semi-sweet chocolate chips, chunks, or chopped baking chocolate (divided)

Gather all ingredients. Preheat the oven to 350°F. Line 8*8 baking dish with parchment paper or spray with non stick baking spray and set aside.

In a medium sized bowl, melt the butter in 15 second increments (so it doesnt explode) until fully melted

Add in granulated sugar and whisk to combined.

Next add in the eggs and vanilla. Whisk until incorporated.

Sift in the cocoa powder, salt and flour.

Stir using a wooden spoon or rubber spatula.

Add in 1 1/2 cup of the chocolate (chips, chunks or chopped pieces) and fold together with the rubber spatula.

Pour into the baking dish.

Add the remaining chocolate to the top and lightly press into the mixture.

Bake for 25-30 mins (until the edges are set and a toothpick comes out with a few crumbs but no batter) Allow to cool completely, then slice and serve.

Baking Buddy Tip

Toothpick testing = brownie brilliance!
Stick a toothpick in the center of your brownies to check doneness.

- If it comes out with a few moist crumbs, they're ready! ✅
- ❌ If there's wet batter, bake a little longer.
- ❌ If it's totally clean, you may have overbaked them—uh-oh, dry brownies!

Science Fact: Brownies keep cooking after they're out of the oven. That's called carryover heat, and it's why we stop baking while they're still a little gooey inside!

Temperature Check: Double Chunk Brownies

Brownies baked? Chocolate melted? Let's see what you learned while mixing up this rich and fudgy recipe!

Why do we melt the butter in short bursts (15 seconds at a time) instead of all at once? *Hint: Think about what happens if you overheat butter in the microwave!*

_____

_____

What does it mean to "fold" in the chocolate chunks—and why do we do it gently?

_____

_____

How do you know when your brownies are done baking? What should the toothpick look like?

_____

_____

What happened to the chocolate you added on top before baking? Did it melt, stay visible, or create chunks on top?

_____

_____

VANILLA BEAN CUPCAKES

SERVING SIZE: 24

PREP: 15 MINUTES

BAKE:20 MINUTES

Review the recipe below and create this on your own. Once completed, answer the questions in the "Temperature Check" section.

BUTTERMILK VANILLA CUPCAKES

EQUIPMENT

- Stand mixer with paddle attachment (or hand mixer)
- Whisk
- Large bowl
- Medium bowl or large glass measuring cup
- Rubber spatula
- 12-count cupcake pan * 2
- Cupcake liners (paper, not aluminum)

INGREDIENTS

For the Cupcakes:
- 2 ½ cups cake flour
- 2 ½ teaspoons baking powder
- 1 teaspoon salt
- ½ cup unsalted butter, room temperature
- ½ cup vegetable oil
- 1 ½ cups granulated sugar
- 4 large eggs, room temperature
- 1 tablespoon vanilla bean paste or 2 tablespoons vanilla extract
- 1 ⅓ cups buttermilk

**For a complete guide on buttercream frosting
Visit: https://teachmehowtobake.com/art-of-buttercream/**

Gather all ingredients. Preheat the oven to 350°F.

In the bowl of a stand mixer fitted with a paddle attachment beat the softened butter and oil together until they become smooth, about 3 minutes.

With the mixture running on medium-low, slowly add the granulated sugar. Beat on high until the mixture is light and fluffy

Add the eggs in one at a time and making sure to mix each time. Then add in the vanilla and beat well

TEACH ME HOW TO BAKE

Add half the dry ingredients, then buttermilk and repeat.

Whip until combined, the batter should be fluffy.

Use a cookie Scoop to add into the liners no more than 3/4 of the way.

Bake for 18-20 minutes, or until a toothpick inserted in the center comes out mostly clean

TEACH ME HOW TO BAKE

Allow the cupcakes to cool completely before frosting.

Add frosting of choice to a pastry bag fit with a large star tip (1M) and frost the cooled cupcakes.

Baking Buddy Tip from Logan Berry

Want cupcakes that rise evenly and bake like a pro? Here's how!

- Only fill each cupcake liner ¾ of the way—that gives the batter room to rise without overflowing or sinking.
- Leave space between cupcakes by filling every other cup in your pan. This helps the heat flow evenly around each cupcake, so they all bake at the same rate.

Science fact: Overfilled cupcakes trap steam, which can push the batter over the top—or cause it to collapse in the middle. Less is more when it comes to fluffy results!

Temperature Check: Buttermilk Vanilla Bean Cupcakes

You've mixed, scooped, and frosted—now let's see what you've learned along the way!

Why is it important to use room temperature butter in this recipe? What happens if it's too cold or too melted? *Hint: Think about texture and rise!*

_____

_____

What does the recipe mean when it says to mix until the batter is "light and fluffy"? How can you tell when it's ready?

_____

_____

How full should you fill the cupcake liners—and what might happen if you fill them too high?

_____

_____

Describe how your cupcakes looked and smelled after baking. Did they rise evenly? Were they golden or pale?

_____

_____

BUTTERSWIM BISCUITS

SERVING SIZE: 9

PREP: 10 MINUTES

BAKE: 20 MINUTES

Review the recipe below and create this on your own. Once completed, answer the questions in the "Temperature Check" section.

BUTTERSWIM BISCUITS

EQUIPMENT

- Measuring Cups and Spoons
- 8*8 baking dish
- Wooden Spoon

INGREDIENTS

- 1 stick unsalted butter
- 2 ½ cups all-purpose flour, scooped and leveled
- 4 teaspoons granulated sugar
- 4 teaspoons baking powder
- 2 teaspoons salt
- 2 cups buttermilk

Hot butter = crispy biscuit edges!

When you pour dough into melted butter, it fries the edges just enough to make them golden and crunchy—while the inside stays soft and fluffy.
Butter's doing **triple duty**:
flavor, texture, and non-stick magic!

Gather all ingredients.
Preheat the oven to 425°F

Place a stick of butter in the
pan and melt it for 4-5
mins, do not let it brown.

Add flour, sugar, baking
powder and salt to a bowl a

Mix all the dry ingredients
together with a whisk or
very carefully with a
wooden spoon

Add in the buttermilk and mix with a wooden spoon until we'll incorporated.

Remove the pan from the oven and carefully add the batter on top

Bake for 18-20 mins until golden brown

Slice the biscuits and serve while still hot.

Temperature Check: Butterswim Biscuits

You just made biscuits that swim in butter—how cool is that?! Let's check in on what you learned while baking

Why do we melt the butter in the baking dish before adding the biscuit batter? *Hint: What does the butter do to the outside of the biscuits?*

_____

_____

What tool did you use to mix the dough—and how did you know when to stop mixing?

_____

_____

What did you notice when you poured the biscuit batter into the melted butter? What happened as it baked?

_____

_____

Describe the look, smell, or texture of your biscuits when they came out of the oven. *Were they golden? Crispy on the edges? Soft in the middle?*

_____

_____

CHOCOLATE CHIP COOKIES

SERVING SIZE: 24

PREP: 12 MINUTES

BAKE: 12 MINUTES

Review the recipe below and create this on your own. Once completed, answer the questions in the "Temperature Check" section.

CHOCOLATE CHIP COOKIES

EQUIPMENT

- Measuring Cups and Spoons
- Stand or Hand Mixer
- Cookie Scoop
- Baking Sheet
- Parchment Paper

INGREDIENTS

- 1/2 cup butter, room temperature
- 1/2 cup granulated sugar
- 1/2 cup light brown sugar
- 1 egg, room temperature
- 2 tsp vanilla extract
- 1 3/4 cup bread flour (can use all-purpose flour)
- 1/2 tsp baking soda
- 1/2 tsp salt
- 2 cups milk chocolate chips

Gather all ingredients.
Preheat the oven to 350°F
Line two sheet pans with
parchement paper.

Place the softended butter,
granulated sugar and
brown sugar in your mixing
bowl.

Using a stand mixer with the
paddle attachment, (or a
hand mixer), cream the
ingredients until light and
fluffy at low speed.

Add the egg and vanilla
extract and blend at low
speed until combined.

In a separate bowl, whisk together the flour, baking soda, and salt.

Gradually add the flour to the butter mixture and mix until just combined.

Finally, stir in the chocolate chips until they are evenly distributed throughout the cookie dough.

Use the cookie scooper to even portion out cookie dough.

Drop rounded tablespoons of cookie dough onto an ungreased baking sheet, leaving some space between each cookie.

Bake in the preheated oven for about 10-12 minutes or until the edges are golden but the centers are still soft. Allow the cookies to cool for 5 minutes on the baking sheet before transferring to a wire rack to cool completely.

Baking Buddy Tip from our baking scientist

Want your cookies to stay soft for days?
Put a slice of fresh bread inside the cookie container!

Here's the science:
Cookies slowly lose moisture and get hard over time—but bread gives up its moisture first. The cookies absorb the moisture from the bread, staying soft while the bread turns dry and hard. Just remember to switch out the bread every day so it doesn't get moldy!

Temperature Check: Chocolate Chip Cookies

Let's check your cookie confidence!

What does it mean to "cream" butter and sugar—and how do you know when it's ready? *Hint: Think about texture and color!*

_____

_____

Why do we mix the dry ingredients in a separate bowl before adding them to the wet ingredients?

_____

_____

What did you notice about your cookies as they baked? Did they spread out, puff up, or change color?

_____

_____

Describe how your cookies felt or tasted once they cooled. Were the edges crisp or soft? What about the middle?

_____

_____

TEACH ME HOW TO BAKE

CRESCENT ROLL QUICHE

SERVING SIZE: 8

PREP: 10 MINUTES

BAKE: 25 MINUTES

Review the recipe below and create this on your own. Once completed, answer the questions in the "Temperature Check" section.

CRESCENT ROLL QUICHE

EQUIPMENT

- Cupcake/Muffin Tin
- Bowls
- Whisk or Fork
- Glass Measuring Cup, optional

INGREDIENTS

- 4 large eggs
- 1 package of crescent roll dough
- ¼ cup shredded cheddar cheese
- ¼ cup shredded mozzarella
- ¼ cup turkey sausage (or any cooked sausage)
- ¼ tsp black pepper
- ¼ tsp salt
- Non-Stick Baking Spray

Gather all ingredients. Preheat the oven to 375°F. Spray the inside of the baking tin with nonstick spray.

Unwrap the crescent roll dough. Add one to each muffin tin, making sure to press it together to cover any gaps.

Crack the eggs into a bowl or liquid measuring cup.

Add in salt and pepper, mix well.

Add breakfast meat and cheese to each cup.

Add 4-5 tablespoons of egg mixture on top. (top with additional cheese if you want)

Bake for 20-25 mins, until a knife inserted in the center comes out clean.

Serve with your favorite breakfast foods and enjoy!

Temperature Check:
Quick & Easy Crescent Roll Quiche

Why do we press the crescent dough into the muffin tin before adding the filling? What could happen if we don't? *Hint: Think about leaks or holes!*

_____

_____

How can you tell when your quiche is done baking? What tool do we use to check it?

_____

_____

What was your favorite part to add—eggs, cheese, sausage, or something else? Why did you choose it?

_____

_____

How did your quiches look and smell after baking? Were the tops golden? Was the filling firm or still soft?

_____

_____

SUGAR COOKIE BARS

SERVING SIZE: 12

PREP: 10 MINUTES

BAKE: 25 MINUTES

Review the recipe below and create this on your own. Once completed, answer the questions in the "Temperature Check" section.

SUGAR COOKIE BARS WITH FLUFFY FROSTING

EQUIPMENT

- Stand mixer with paddle attachment (or hand mixer)
- 8x8-inch baking pan
- Parchment paper
- Mixing bowls
- Rubber spatula

INGREDIENTS

For the Cookie Bars:

- 1¼ cups all-purpose flour
- 1 tablespoon cornstarch
- ½ teaspoon baking powder
- ¼ teaspoon baking soda
- ¼ teaspoon salt
- ½ cup unsalted butter (room temperature)
- ½ cup granulated sugar
- 1 large egg
- 2 teaspoons vanilla extract

For the Frosting:

- ½ cup unsalted butter (room temperature)
- ¼ cup cream cheese (room temperature)
- 2 cups powdered sugar
- 1 teaspoon vanilla extract
- 2 tablespoons heavy cream
- 1 drop pink gel food coloring (optional)
- Sprinkles for topping

Preheat your oven to 350°F. Line your 8x8-inch baking pan with parchment paper, folding it to fit. This makes it easy to lift the cookie bars out after frosting.

In a large bowl, use a stand mixer or hand mixer to beat the butter and granulated sugar on medium speed until the mixture is light and fluffy (about 2–3 minutes).

Mix in the egg and vanilla extract until fully combined.

Slowly add the flour mixture to the wet ingredients and mix until everything is just combined

Do not overmix- stop when the flour disappears. Press the cookie dough evenly into the prepared pan.

Bake for 20–25 minutes, or until the edges are lightly golden and the center is set Let cool completely (20-30 mins).

In a large bowl, beat the butter and cream cheese together until smooth and creamy.

TEACH ME HOW TO BAKE

Gradually add the powdered sugar, vanilla extract, and heavy cream. Beat until light and fluffy. If using, add 1 drop of pink gel food coloring and mix until evenly colored.

Spread the frosting evenly over the cooled cookie bar. Top with sprinkles for extra fun!

Slice into 12 bars and enjoy!

Cocoa Cookie's Baking Breakdown

Baking Science: Why Do We Use Cornstarch? Cornstarch softens the texture of the cookie bars, making them extra tender and chewy. It works with the flour to help create that soft bite without making the bars crumbly!

Why should butter be at room temperature? Room temp butter blends better with sugar and cream cheese—making your frosting extra smooth and fluffy. Cold butter stays chunky, and melted butter? Way too runny!

Tip: Let your butter sit out for 30–45 minutes before you bake. That's the sweet spot!

Temperature Check:
Sugar Cookie Bars with Fluffy Frosting

Those bars are baked, frosted, and sprinkled—now let's check what you learned while making them!

What does "cream the butter and sugar" mean, and how do you know when you've done it right?

_____

_____

Why do we let the cookie bars cool completely before adding the frosting? *Hint: What might happen if the frosting goes on too soon?*

_____

_____

What does cornstarch do in this recipe, and how does it change the texture of the bars?

_____

_____

What tools or steps helped you press the dough evenly into the pan? Was it easy or tricky?

_____

_____

SHEETPAN PANCAKES

SERVING SIZE: 12

PREP: 10 MINUTES

BAKE: 18 MINUTES

Review the recipe below and create this on your own. Once completed, answer the questions in the "Temperature Check" section.

SHEETPAN PANCAKES

EQUIPMENT

- Large Mixing Bowl
- Rubber spatula
- Whisk
- Measuring Cups
- Measuring Spoons
- Parchment Paper
- Baking Sheet (18*13)

INGREDIENTS

- 4 cups Bisquick
- 4 large eggs
- 2 cups whole milk
- 1 tablespoon vanilla
- Chocolate Chips or Fruit, optional

MAKE YOUR OWN BISQUICK

You'll need:
- 6 cups all-purpose flour
- 3 Tbsp baking powder
- 1 Tbsp salt
- 1 cup vegetable shortening (cubed)

Let's mix it up:
1. Add the flour, baking powder, and salt to a food processor.
2. Pulse for 15 seconds.
3. Add shortening and pulse again until it looks like cornmeal.
4. Store in an airtight container in the fridge for up to 3 months.

Gather all ingredients. Preheat the oven to 425°F. Spray a standard half sheet pan with nonstick spray (13×18) and set aside.

Add bisquick, eggs, vanilla and milk to a large bowl

Whisk until well combined.

Pour the batter into the prepared baking tray and spread out with a spatula.

Add your favorite toppings to the top of the batter. Be as creative as you'd like!

Bake for 15-18 minutes or until golden brown.

Let your pancakes cool for a few minutes (about 3-4) before asking for help to slice them.

Serve with your favorite breakfast foods and enjoy!

Temperature Check: Sheet Pan Pancakes

Why do we preheat the oven before we bake—and how do we know it's ready?

_____

_____

What tool did you use to mix the batter—and why is it important not to overmix pancake batter?

_____

_____

What happened to your pancake as it baked? Did it puff up, stay flat, or turn golden? Describe what you noticed.

_____

_____

Which kitchen stations did you use for this recipe? *Hint: Think about where you mixed, where you baked, and where you prepped your pan.)*

_____

_____

STRAWBERRY MUFFINS

SERVING SIZE: 10

PREP: 10 MINUTES

BAKE: 25 MINUTES

Review the recipe below and create this on your own. Once completed, answer the questions in the "Temperature Check" section.

STRAWBERRY MUFFINS

EQUIPMENT

- Large Mixing Bowl
- Hand Mixer or Whisk
- Softer
- 12 ct muffin/cupcake tray

INGREDIENTS

- ¼ cup unsalted butter, melted
- ¾ cup granulated sugar
- 1 egg
- 1 teaspoon vanilla extract
- ½ cup whole milk
- 1 ¼ cup all-purpose flour, scooped and leveled
- 1 ½ teaspoons baking powder
- 5-7 strawberries, diced

Why chop strawberries small before baking?

Big fruit chunks can make muffins too wet in the middle!
  When you chop strawberries into tiny pieces, they spread out better, bake evenly, and give you juicy bites in every muffin.

TEACH ME HOW TO BAKE

Gather all ingredients.
Preheat the oven to 350°F.
Prepare the muffin tin with
liners and set aside

Add the butter to a
microwave-safe bowl and
melt in 15 sec increments
(this prevents it from
exploding), then add sugar
and whisk.

Add in the egg, milk and
vanilla and mix well.

Sift in the flour, baking
powder and salt.

Mix wet and dry together until incorporated, then add strawberries.

Fold in with a spatula

Using an ice cream scooper, add even amounts to the muffins tin.

Bake for 20-25 mins.

Temperature Check: Strawberry Muffins

Your muffins are baked, fluffy, and full of sweet strawberry goodness! Let's check in on your kitchen know-how.

Why do we melt the butter in short bursts instead of all at once in the microwave?

_____

_____

What tool did you use to portion the muffin batter, and why is it important to keep them even?

_____

_____

How did your muffins change in the oven? Did they rise, get golden on top, or smell amazing?

_____

_____

What did you notice about the strawberries in your muffins after baking?

_____

_____

Which kitchen stations did you use for this recipe?

_____

_____

YOU DID IT, BAKER!

Congratulations! You've mixed, measured, and baked your way through Teach Me How to Bake—and we're so proud of you.

Whether it was your first cookie or your tenth muffin, you've taken real steps toward becoming a confident home baker. You learned the basics, followed recipes, and practiced safe, smart baking. **That's a big deal!**

Just remember:

- **Every great baker starts somewhere**
- **Mistakes are part of the fun**
- **Practice makes progress (and sweet memories)**

We'll be cheering you on—every recipe, every time.

Keep mixing up magic!

With pride and sprinkles,

Cocoa Cookie, Graham C. Moore, Honey Blu, Logan Berry, Bramble Berry & Benedict Waffle

The Baking Buddies Crew

TEACH ME HOW TO BAKE

KIMBERLY HOUSTON

> I believe the kitchen is more than a place to cook—it's a classroom for life.

Chef Kimberly Houston is a Le Cordon Bleu-trained pastry chef, certified baking instructor, and curriculum designer with over a decade of experience helping kids and families build confidence in the kitchen. Her passion is blending baking, science, and joyful learning into hands-on experiences that stick.

She holds two Master's degrees—in Education and Transformational Leadership—and is certified in Child Nutrition, Instructional Design, and Entrepreneurship.

As the founder of Houston Collective, Kimberly leads multiple inspiring brands with Teach Me How to Bake, a baking education company with online classes and trainings for culinary educators at the helm.

Join the academy

The learning doesn't have to end! It can continue Sweet friends!

Join the Teach Me How to Bake Academy at the link below.

teachmehowtobake.com/academy

GLOSSARY

GLOSSARY

A

All-Purpose Flour
A white flour made from hard winter wheat and is versatile wheat flour with moderate protein content.

Almond Flour
One of the most common gluten-free flours, also known as Almond meal, is made from almonds that have been blanched, meaning the skin has been removed.

Arrowroot Flour
Less commonly known, but it is gluten and grain-free. It can be used as a thickener or mixed with other flours to create bread products.

B

Baking Sheets
Long rectangular-shaped plates that are used to hold small food items in place to bake inside of an oven.

Batter
A term used to describe an unbaked mixture that is thin enough to pour or scoop but cannot be rolled out like a dough.

Bread Flour
A white flour made from hard spring wheat which has a higher protein content than the wheat used to mill all-purpose flour.

Brown Sugar
A granulated sugar with molasses added to it that comes in many colors.

Buckwheat Flour
A sturdy flour that is rich in fiber and nutrients and helps the body fight off inflammation with built-in antioxidants.

Bundt Pan
A baking container that is used for baking cakes designed to have grooved edges or small, circular openings in the middle for decorating purposes.

C

Cabinets

A fixture inside the kitchen that stores objects such as bowls, cups, pots, pans, blenders, toasters and so much more.

Cake Flour

A very finely milled white flour made from soft winter wheat.

Caramelize

A term used to refer to the change sugar goes through when it is heated and allowed to brown.

Coconut Flour

Coconut flour is made from dried coconut meat and offers a mild coconut flavor.

Cookie Cutters

A small, thin kitchen utensil predominately made of metal or hard plastic is used to cut out flattened dough into various shapes and designs for making cookies.

Cooking Station

A section of the kitchen where food items can be prepared either over an open flame or inside of a compartment before being served.

Cookware

Containers such as pots, pans, skillets, griddles, and woks that can be used on top of a stove to prepare meals inside of.

Countertop

A surface inside of the kitchen where food items are prepared and processed.

Creaming Method

A term used to describe the process of beating together solid fat with sugar.

Cupcake Liners

A small circular-shaped item, usually made from very thin paper or metal foil, with triangular grooves around the circular design used to hold the batter in place inside a muffin tin while baking inside the oven.

Cut-In Method

A term used to describe the process of having pieces of solid fat, like butter or shortening, worked into flour and other dry ingredients until the fat starts to coat the flour.

D

Dishes

A container, usually square, circular, or 'squoval' (a square shape with circular corners on each side instead of pointy triangular sides), shaped that is used to prepare or serve food.

Dishwasher

An appliance used to clean and wash dishes, glasses, storage containers, silverware, and other dishwasher-safe items.

Dough

A term used to describe a thick unbaked mixture that can be rolled out or shaped by hand.

Drawers

A moveable fixture inside the kitchen where you can store items such as silverware, utensils, and other kitchen items.

Dry-Ingredient Measuring Cup

A kitchen utensil that measures dry ingredients in containers that resemble smaller-sized cups.

E

Electrical Socket

A fixture that provides electricity to an electronic device.

Emulsion

A term used to describe the process of mixing two ingredients together by force that are normally unmixable, like mixing oil and water or water and fat together.

F

Ferment

A term used to describe the process of yeast feeding on sugars and starches present in yeast dough.

Food Preparation Station

A section of the kitchen where food items can be chopped, mixed, blended, or combined with other ingredients before being served.

Folding

A term used to describe the technique used to incorporate two mixtures together in a very delicate way.

Freezer

An appliance that is used to store food and liquids for later use, but at extremely low temperatures.

G

Glassware

Containers that are used to serve liquids, such as water, juice, soda, and other drinks.

Gluten

A term used to describe the proteins found in wheat flour that are hydrated and bond together, forming what is called 'gluten.'

Granulated Sugar

A refined sugar that is the most common type of sugar in baking and is white in color.

Grater

A grater is a rectangle-shaped kitchen utensil with many sharp downward-facing grooves on its surface that are used to cut or grate food items into small pieces.

H

Hand Mixer

A smaller electronic machine that has two wire whisks (or other mixing utensils) attached to a motorized chamber that you hold with your hand.

K

Kitchen Appliance

A piece of equipment, usually electronic, that is used for the preparation of food items.

Kitchen Scale

A kitchen scale is a portable device that is used to weigh both ingredients and food items.

Knead

A term used to describe the process of working or pressing into a dough with your hands to help create layers to baked goods.

L

Leaven

A term used to describe the chemical reaction process between acid and soda when producing carbon dioxide to leaven, or rise, the dough.

Liquid Measuring Cup

A kitchen utensil that measures liquid in containers that resemble cups.

Loaf Pan

A small rectangular-shaped container used to hold bread dough in place for the process of baking bread, or meats like meatloaf, inside of an oven.

M

Measuring Cup

A kitchen utensil that is used to measure various amounts of ingredients for the purpose of meal preparation.

Microwave

A small or medium-sized electronic machine that uses heat waves and a motor-powered circular tray to heat up food items in a short period of time.

Mixing Bowls

A circular container that is used to mix and blend ingredients, wet or dry, together for the purpose of meal preparation.

Muffin Tin

A rectangular-shaped baking container with multiple circles, or molds, in rows used for baking muffins, cupcakes, or other muffin-like designs.

O

Oven

A large piece of equipment that heats up food items inside an enclosed compartment. It is sometimes referred to as a stove.

Oven Thermometer

Sometimes called a meat thermometer, it is a small circular device, usually made of metal material, that is used to monitor the temperature of food items inside of an oven.

P

Pastry Flour (Whole Wheat Pastry Flour)

A flour milled from soft white wheat and mainly used for cookies and pies.

Pantry

A fixture inside the kitchen that stores many objects such as food, storage containers, utensils, dishes, cookware, kitchen appliances, glassware, and even cleaning supplies.

Peaks

A term used to refer to the stiffness of whipped cream or whipped egg whites.

Piping Bags

A kitchen utensil that is used in the process of decorating baked goods.

Powdered Sugar

Also called confectioners sugar, icing, or 10x sugar, is a very finely ground white sugar used to make icings and frostings.

Proofing

A term used to describe the final process of yeast dough rising before it is baked.

R

Refrigerator

An appliance that is used to store food and liquids for later use.

Rolling Pin

A kitchen utensil that is used to flatten or mold the dough into various sizes.

Rubber/Metal Spatula

A small handheld kitchen utensil that is used to stir or mix ingredients together inside of a container or cooking dish.

S

Sanding Sugar

A very coarse type of granulated sugar that is kept clear or sometimes colored in a variety of colors.

Service Station

A section of the kitchen where food items can be placed on plates or inside of containers before being served.

Self-Rising Flour

A variety of white flour that has salt and baking powder already combined into it.

Sifter

A handheld kitchen utensil that is used to break up dry ingredients to remove any unwanted items that may be hidden inside.

Silverware

Items that can be used to eat a meal with, such as a fork, spoon, or knife.

Sink

A circular-shaped structure that is used to wash and clean items, such as dishes, vegetables, cooking items, and hands.

Softened Butter

A term used to describe the process of cooling butter to a room temperature, between 68-72 degrees Fahrenheit, to be soft enough when making yeast bread or pastries.

Sorghum Flour

Finely ground flour that is used as a gluten-free alternative for baking.

Stand Mixer

A large electronic machine with a circular metal bowl and a whisk, held together by a stand capable of blending large amounts of ingredients together at various speed levels over long periods of time.

Storage Container

An object usually square, rectangular, or round, used to house items that are not currently being utilized inside of the kitchen.

Storage Station

A section of the kitchen where food items can be sealed in air-tight containers until they are either prepared or served.

Stove

A piece of equipment that heats up and is used to prepare meals in pots, pans, or other stove-safe cookware.

Sugar in the Raw:

A very coarse-textured sugar that has been minimally processed and used in batters. Raw Sugar is also called turbinado sugar.

Super Fine Sugar

A more finely ground granulated sugar that is also known as castor or caster sugar and is commonly used for batters and doughs.

U

Utensils

Items that can be used to eat or prepare food with.

W

Washing Station

A section of the kitchen where food items can be cleaned and washed before being prepared.

White Flour

A soft fine flour made from the endosperm of wheat that is used in traditional baking.

Whole Wheat

A fine flour made of wheat grain that is used in traditional baking.

Wire Rack

A square-shaped kitchen utensil that is used to cool off baked goods once they are removed from a heated container.

Wire Whisk

A small handheld utensil that has a combination of wire loops at one end and is held together at its base with a handle that is primarily used for blending, or whipping, ingredients together usually for a short period of time.

Wooden cup

A kitchen utensil, similar to that of a measuring cup, that is used to measure various amounts of ingredients for the purpose of meal preparation.

Z

Zester

A small handheld kitchen utensil that is used to shave or peel pieces of layers from fruits, like oranges and lemons, that can later be assembled as a topping or a key flavor for a prepared meal.

ANSWER KEY

Skill Check-In - Baking Basics

You've already learned so much! Let's take a moment to see how much you remember before we jump into our next chapter.

What is baking, and what are some foods you can bake?

Answer: Baking is cooking food using dry heat—usually in an oven. Foods you can bake include cookies, cakes, breads, and muffins.

What does a baker do?

Answer: A baker prepares food using baking methods like mixing, shaping, and heating. Anyone can be a baker with practice and the right tools!.

What happens inside the oven when you bake your cookies?

Answer: The butter melted, the dough spread, the leaveners helped it rise, and the outside turned golden as the cookies baked.

What do step-by-step recipe photos help you do?

Answer: They show what each part of the recipe should look like, so you can follow along more confidently and make sure you're on track.

What are some of the tools bakers use to make cookies like the ones you just made?

Answer: Tools include a mixer, sifter, baking sheet, parchment paper, and cookie scoop.

Skill Check-In - Kitchen Safety Terms

Let's test how well you remember the safety terms and actions we've learned!

Match each safety rule or kitchen item with the correct description.

Write the letter that matches each numbered item. **Answer Key**

1. Wash your hands — E
2. Tie back long hair — G
3. Ask an adult for help — C
4. Wipe up spills right away — A
5. Clean up broken glass — I
6. Countertop — B
7. Cabinet — J
8. Kitchen appliance — H
9. Outlet — F
10. Ask for help — D

Skill Check-In - Tools & Terms

Can you find and circle all the tools used in this recipe?

SUGAR COOKIES

EQUIPMENT

- Parchment Paper
- Baking Sheets
- Hand or Stand Mixer
- Cookie Scoop, optional

INGREDIENTS

- 2 ¾ cups all-purpose flour
- 1 teaspoon baking soda
- ½ teaspoon baking powder
- 1 cup butter, softened
- 1 ½ cups white sugar
- 1 egg
- 1 teaspoon vanilla extract

INSTRUCTIONS

- Gather all ingredients. Preheat the oven to 375 degrees F
- Stir flour, baking soda, and baking powder together in a **small bowl**.
- Beat sugar and butter together in a large bowl with an electric **mixer** until smooth.
- Beat in egg and vanilla.
- Gradually add in the flour mixture.
- Roll dough into walnut-sized balls and place 2 inches apart onto ungreased or **parchment-lined baking sheets.**
- Bake in the preheated **oven** until edges are golden, 8 to 10 minutes.
- Cool on **the baking sheets** briefly before removing to a wire rack to cool completely

TEACH ME HOW TO BAKE

Skill Check-In - Tools & Terms

What's the difference between a hand mixer and a stand mixer?

Answer: A hand mixer is held in your hand for smaller batches. A stand mixer sits on the counter and mixes bigger batches with different speeds

When should you use a rubber spatula instead of a whisk?

Answer: A rubber spatula is best for scraping and folding gently. A whisk is for blending and adding air.

Why is it important to level your dry ingredients when measuring?

Answer: Leveling ensures your measurements are accurate—too much flour can make things dry!

What does the cut-in method do to cold butter in recipes?

Answer: The cut-in method keeps butter cold so it melts in the oven, creating flaky layers.

Can you explain what "softened butter" means and why it's used in baking?

Answer: Softened butter is room temperature (not melted) and helps trap air for soft textures.

Skill Check-In - Measurements

Let's pause and see how much you've learned about measuring the right way—because great bakers don't guess, they measure with confidence!

What's the difference between packed brown sugar and loose brown sugar?

Answer: Packed is pressed down tight. Loose is scooped and left fluffy. Packed gives you more sugar in the same cup.

Why is it important to read the whole recipe before you start baking?

Answer: It helps you know what to do, what tools you need, and how long it'll take—no surprises!

How can you tell the difference between a liquid measuring cup and a dry measuring cup?

Answer: Liquid cups are clear with a spout.
Dry cups are solid and made to fill to the top and level off.

How do you measure dry ingredients like flour the right way?

Answer: Spoon it in, then level it off with the back of a knife. Don't pack it down!

Why is precision so important when baking?

Answer: Because baking is like science—too much or too little can change how things bake or taste.

Skill Check-In - Baking Science Review

What does flour do in a recipe—and what happens when it mixes with water?

Answer: Flour builds structure in baked goods. When flour mixes with water, it forms gluten

How is brown sugar different from white sugar, and why does that matter in baking?

Answer: Brown sugar has molasses added to it, which makes it moister and chewier than white sugar.

What are two reasons eggs are important in baking?

Answer: Eggs help bind ingredients, trap air for fluffiness, and add moisture and richness. They also help baked goods rise and hold their shape.

Can you name and explain the three types of leavening agents?

Answer: Chemical leaveners (like baking soda or baking powder) release bubbles during a reaction.
 • Biological leaveners (like yeast) create bubbles slowly as they eat sugar.
 • Mechanical leaveners (like whipped eggs or cream) trap air by beating or whipping.

Why is it important to choose the right type of flour for your recipe?

Answer: Different flours have different protein levels, which affects gluten

Temperature Check: 4-in-1 Sheet Pan Cookies

What does "fold until mostly combined" mean, and why don't we want to overmix the dough?

Answer: *"Folding means gently mixing with a spatula to keep the dough soft. Overmixing makes cookies tough.*

Which of the four cookie flavors was your favorite to make —and why?

Answer: *Answers will vary—look for one flavor (Chocolate Chip, Funfetti, Cookies 'n' Cream, or Double Chocolate) and a fun reason (sprinkles, melted chunks, Oreo pieces, etc.).*

What did you notice about the texture of your cookies after they cooled? Did they puff up or settle down?

Answer: *Cookies may puff up, then settle. Kids might notice they're chewy, soft in the middle, or crisp on the edges.*

Which kitchen stations did you use while making this recipe?

Answer:
- *Prep Station – to measure ingredients and portion the dough*
- *Mixing Station – to stir and fold in mix-ins*
- *Cooking/Baking Station – for spreading the dough on the sheet pan and placing it in the oven*
- *Clean-Up Station – to wash bowls, utensils, and the pan*

Temperature Check: Classic Banana Bread

Why do we mash the bananas before adding them to the batter instead of adding them whole? *Hint: Think about mixing and texture!*

Answer: Mashing the bananas makes them easier to mix into the batter evenly. Whole bananas wouldn't blend well and could leave big, wet chunks that affect the texture of the bread.

What tool did you use to combine the dry and wet ingredients —and why is it important not to overmix?

Answer: A rubber spatula is used to gently mix the ingredients. Overmixing can make the bread tough instead of soft because it activates too much gluten.

What did your banana bread look, smell, or feel like when it came out of the oven? *Was it golden? Did the top feel firm? How did it smell?*

Answer: It should be golden brown on top, with a firm crust. It likely smelled sweet and nutty from the bananas and walnuts. (Encourage sensory language: "warm," "crackly top," "banana smell," etc.)

Did you use buttermilk or whole milk in your batter? How do you think it helped the bread?

Answer: Either milk adds moisture and helps soften the texture. Buttermilk also adds a little tang and reacts with baking soda to help the bread rise.

TEACH ME HOW TO BAKE

Temperature Check: Double Chunk Brownies

Brownies baked? Chocolate melted? Let's see what you learned while mixing up this rich and fudgy recipe!

Why do we melt the butter in short bursts?

Answer: To keep the butter from overheating and exploding or bubbling over in the microwave. Short bursts give you better control.

What does it mean to fold in the chocolate—and why gently?

Answer: Folding means mixing slowly and carefully so the batter stays smooth. Stirring too hard can make brownies tough or overmix the batter.

How do you know when brownies are done?

Answer: Stick a toothpick in the center. If it comes out with a few moist crumbs but no wet batter, they're ready!

What happened to the chocolate on top?

Answer: It may melt slightly, stay chunky, or create a crackly chocolate layer—it depends on the type of chocolate and how long it baked.

Temperature Check:
Buttermilk Vanilla Bean Cupcakes

You've mixed, scooped, and frosted—now let's see what you've learned along the way!

Why is it important to use room temperature butter in this recipe?

Answer: Room temperature butter traps air as it's creamed with sugar, helping the cupcakes rise and turn out soft and fluffy. Cold butter won't mix well, and melted butter won't trap air at all.

What does "light and fluffy" batter look like—and how do you know it's ready?

Answer: The batter should look pale and feel airy when stirred. You know it's ready when the sugar and butter mixture is no longer grainy and has lightened in color.

How full should you fill the cupcake liners—and what happens if you go over?

Answer: Fill each liner no more than ¾ full. If you overfill, the batter can overflow or sink in the middle. It also may bake unevenly.

Describe how your cupcakes looked and smelled after baking

Answer: They should be lightly golden on top, slightly domed, and have a sweet, buttery vanilla scent. This question encourages sensory awareness —look for words like fluffy, soft, golden, or fragrant.

Temperature Check: Butterswim Biscuits

Why do we melt the butter in the baking dish before adding the biscuit batter?

Answer: The butter coats the bottom and sides of the pan, helping the biscuits get crispy and golden on the outside while staying soft in the middle. It also prevents sticking.

What tool did you use to mix the dough—and how did you know when to stop mixing?

Answer: A wooden spoon is used to stir the dough. You stop when all the ingredients are just combined—no dry flour left, but don't overmix, or the biscuits can turn out dense.

What did you notice when you poured the biscuit batter into the melted butter?

Answer: The butter bubbled around the edges and began to coat the top of the dough. As it baked, the butter soaked into the bottom and gave it a buttery, golden crust.

Describe the look, smell, or texture of your biscuits.

Answer: Biscuits should be golden brown on top, slightly crisp at the edges, and soft and fluffy inside. They'll smell rich and buttery—maybe even a little sweet from the sugar!

Temperature Check: Chocolate Chip Cookies

Let's check your cookie confidence!

What does it mean to "cream" butter and sugar—and how do you know when it's ready?

Answer: Creaming means mixing softened butter and sugar until the mixture is light and fluffy. This adds air, which helps the cookies rise and spread evenly. It's ready when the color is pale and the texture looks soft and smooth.

Why do we mix the dry ingredients in a separate bowl before adding them to the wet ingredients?

Answer: Mixing dry ingredients separately helps spread the baking soda and salt evenly through the flour, so they don't clump or create uneven spots in the dough.

What did you notice about your cookies as they baked? Did they spread out, puff up, or change color?

Answer: The cookies should spread slightly, puff up a little in the center, and turn golden around the edges. They may flatten more as they cool.

Describe how your cookies felt or tasted once they cooled. Were the edges crisp or soft? What about the middle?

Answer: The edges should be slightly crisp, and the centers soft and chewy. Some might describe them as gooey, melt-in-your-mouth, or firm depending on bake time.

Temperature Check:
Quick & Easy Crescent Roll Quiche

Now that your pancake is baked and ready to eat, let's check in on what you learned!

Why do we press the crescent dough into the muffin tin before adding the filling?

Answer: Pressing the dough into the tin makes a little "crust cup" that holds the egg mixture. If you don't press it in or leave gaps, the eggs can leak out during baking or stick to the pan.

How can you tell when your quiche is done baking? What tool do we use to check it?

Answer: You check by inserting a butter knife or toothpick into the center. If it comes out clean (with no wet egg), the quiche is fully baked.

What was your favorite part to add—eggs, cheese, sausage, or something else?

Answer: Answers will vary. Look for enthusiasm and reasoning like "I love melty cheese!" or "The sausage made it extra flavorful."

How did your quiches look and smell after baking?

Answer: They should be golden on top, slightly puffed, and smell savory. The egg filling should feel firm and not jiggle too much when gently touched.

Temperature Check:
Sugar Cookie Bars with Fluffy Frosting

Those bars are baked, frosted, and sprinkled—now let's check what you learned while making them!

What does "cream the butter and sugar" mean?

Answer: It means mixing them until they're light and fluffy. This helps make the bars soft and gives them a good rise.

Why cool before frosting?

Answer: If the bars are still warm, the frosting will melt and slide off—and nobody wants runny frosting!

What does cornstarch do?

Answer: It helps make the bars extra soft and chewy without falling apart.

What helped you press the dough into the pan?

Answer: A rubber spatula or clean hands! The dough can be sticky, so pressing gently and evenly takes a little patience.

Temperature Check: Sheet Pan Pancakes

Now that your pancake is baked and ready to eat, let's check in on what you learned!

Why do we preheat the oven before we bake—and how do we know it's ready?

Answer: We preheat the oven so it's at the right temperature when the batter goes in. This helps the pancake bake evenly. Most ovens have a light or beep that signals when they're fully preheated.

What tool did you use to mix the batter—and why is it important not to overmix pancake batter?

Answer: A whisk or rubber spatula is used to mix the batter. Overmixing can create too much gluten, which makes pancakes tough instead of light and fluffy.

What happened to your pancake as it baked? Did it puff up, stay flat, or turn golden? Describe what you noticed.

Answer: The pancake should puff up slightly and turn golden brown on top. It may settle a bit as it cools. Kids might also notice bubbles forming or the top becoming firm.

Which kitchen stations did you use for this recipe?

Answer:
- Prep station – for measuring and mixing ingredients
- Cooking station – for baking in the oven
- Clean-up station – for washing dishes or tools
- (You could also mention the service station if the pancake was plated or shared!)

Temperature Check: Strawberry Muffins

Your muffins are baked, fluffy, and full of sweet strawberry goodness! Let's check in on your kitchen know-how:

Why melt butter in short bursts?

Answer: So it doesn't explode! Short bursts keep it from overheating and help melt it gently.

Why use an ice cream scoop?

Answer: They rose, got golden on top, and filled the kitchen with a yummy strawberry smell!

What happened to the strawberries?

Answer: They softened and spread through the muffin, adding flavor and little bursts of fruit in each bite.

Which kitchen stations did you use for this recipe?

Answer:
- Prep Station – Measuring and chopping
- Mixing Station – Combining ingredients
- Baking Station – Using the oven
- Clean-Up Station – Washing bowls and tools